Step by Step

Publisher's Acknowledgment

THE PUBLISHER GRATEFULLY ACKNOWLEDGES the generous help of the Hershey Family Foundation in sponsoring the publication of this book.

Step by Step

Basic Buddhist Meditations

Geshe Namgyal Wangchen

Wisdom Publications • Boston

Wisdom Publications
199 Elm Street
Somerville MA 02144 USA
www.wisdompubs.org

Library of Congress Cataloging-in-Publication Data
Namgyal Wangchen.
 Step by step : basic Buddhist meditations / Namgyal Wangchen.
    p. cm.
 Revision and expansion of: Awakening the mind. 1995.
 ISBN 0-86171-600-0 (pbk. : alk. paper)
 1. Lam-rim. 2. Meditation—Buddhism. I. Namgyal Wangchen. Awakening the
mind. II. Title.
 BQ7645.L35N35 2009
 294.3'4435—dc22
                                    2009008865

13 12 11 10 09
5 4 3 2 1

Cover design by TLJE. Interior design by TLLC. Set in Adobe Garamond 10.75/14.
Previously published under the title *Awakening the Mind*.

Wisdom Publications' books are printed on acid-free paper and meet the guidelines for permanence and durability of the Production Guidelines for Book
Longevity of the Council on Library Resources.

Printed in the United States of America.

♻ This book was produced with environmental mindfulness. We have elected to print
this title on 30% PCW recycled paper. As a result, we have saved the following resources:
14 trees, 4 million BTUs of energy, 1,343 lbs. of greenhouse gases, 6,467 gallons of
water, and 393 lbs. of solid waste. For more information, please visit our website,
www.wisdompubs.org. This paper is also FSC certified. For more information, please
visit www.fscus.org.

Contents

Preface   *vii*

Acknowledgments   *ix*

Introduction   1

Part One: Basic Requirements for the Practice of Meditation

1. The Meaning of the Gradual Path to Enlightenment
   (Lam Rim)   13
2. The Four Significant Qualities of the Gradual Path   21
3. Our Motivation for Practicing Meditation   23
4. The Levels of the Path   29
5. Preparing Ourselves for the Actual Meditation:
   The Six Preliminary Practices   35

Part Two: Meditations on the Initial Level of Inner Development

6. The Precious Human Rebirth   59
7. Awareness of Impermanence   67
8. Taking Refuge in the Three Jewels   73

Part Three: Meditation on the Medium Level of Inner Development

9. The Suffering Nature of Cyclic Existence   85

Part Four: Meditations on the High Level of Inner Development

10. Encouraging Ourselves to Develop Bodhicitta,
    the Mind of Enlightenment   99

11. How to Develop Bodhicitta   107

Part Five: The Six Perfections

12. Encouraging Ourselves to Practice the Bodhisattva Path   135

13. Introducing the Six Perfections   139

14. Meditations on the First Four Perfections   157

15. The Importance of Developing a Single-Pointed Mind,
    the Fifth Perfection   167

16. How to Develop a Single-Pointed Mind   171

17. The Wisdom of Emptiness, the Sixth Perfection   193

18. Meditation on Emptiness   201

19. Meditations on the Three Deities   223

Appendix: Prayers in Tibetan Phonetics and English   227

Glossary   235

About the Author   241

Preface

As we all know, inner, or spiritual, development is very important to our well-being. Outer wealth and inner development, if cultivated together, can bring about a more complete form of happiness.

All spiritual traditions teach methods for developing inner happiness, and Buddhism in particular clearly explains what the root of suffering is and how to eradicate it. It teaches how an undisciplined mind, one full of anger, or attachment, causes suffering, while a disciplined one, imbued with patience, love, and understanding, brings about happiness.

Our mind is naturally influenced by non-virtuous thoughts. If we do not try to subdue and eventually eliminate them, the clear, pure nature of mind cannot manifest. Once this pure nature manifests, our mind is clearly able to perceive what is right from what is wrong; we gain freedom from all non-virtuous thoughts, which cause our suffering, and our actions of body and speech become virtuous. It is therefore essential that we train our mind in order to purify it and thereby reveal its true nature. This is accomplished by means of the Dharma, which teaches the method for altering and shaping our mind.

When a mirror reveals imperfections in our appearance, unless we remove these faults, the mirror has been of little use. Similarly, it is not enough simply to know what is wholesome and what is unwholesome; to practice is essential. As the Buddha has said, we are our own masters. In our daily lives, we must constantly watch over our minds and apply effective methods for removing our non-virtuous ways of thinking. This will definitely bring about progress.

I hope that through this book those who are interested in spiritual practice will derive some benefit.

This book is dedicated to the long life of His Holiness the Dalai Lama, to all great peace-loving leaders of other religions, and to the fulfillment of their great wish for universal peace.

Geshe Namgyal Wangchen
Drepung Loseling Monastery, India

Acknowledgments

First of all I pay homage to my kind spiritual teachers, especially to the highly realized great master, the Venerable Khensur Pema Gyaltsen Rinpoche. It is because of their kindness that I have been able to write this book, in English, based on the traditional practice of profound Mahayana Buddhist meditations. It is my sincere hope that this book may help my dear Western friends overcome any difficulties they might experience because of cultural differences and come to understand the traditional way of practicing meditation.

I am delighted by Wisdom Publications' desire to republish this book in this new edition and under this new title, as it reflects an interest in spirituality in general and in Buddhism in particular. I offer my thanks to Timothy J. McNeill, T.J. MacDuff Stewart, Rod Meade Sperry, and Joe Evans.

Regarding the earlier edition of this book, I would again like to thank Mr. Geoff Jukes, founder of the Meridian Trust, for his kind generosity in sponsoring the publication of this book. I am deeply grateful to my editor, Anila Constance Miller. I also thank Pauline Poulton and Lydia Muell-bauer for their work in typing and editing; the students of Manjushri London Centre for their practical help; and lastly, Robina Courtin and Nick Ribush.

Whatever benefits this book may have are owed to my kind spiritual teachers and dear Dharma friends.

Buddha Shakyamuni

Introduction

Today our material standards of living are high and many of the physical problems that humanity used to face no longer exist. Indeed, the present high standards of material progress have brought us many good things, yet at a deeper level we are facing another type of problem, perhaps even more urgent than ever—the danger of losing our basic human values.

Most of the problems we face are due to the complexity of the human mind. These mind-made problems seem more serious and complicated than material ones; hence people today wonder where these problems come from and how to solve them. Many of us are beginning to realize that material life without an inner or spiritual awareness does not satisfy our needs. We human beings need both material comfort and spiritual awareness; one without the other is incomplete and not harmonious.

All pure spiritual paths show us how to develop our inner virtuous qualities, such as tolerance, love, compassion, and determination. Buddhism, taught by Buddha Shakyamuni more than two and a half thousand years ago, is one of these spiritual paths. It teaches that the fundamental cause of our suffering and problems is our own deluded or undisciplined mind. Therefore, the way to liberate ourself from suffering is by training our own mind. First, awareness of our own suffering is important; when we see our suffering at a deep level we are able to see what the cause is: our deluded states of mind and the unskillful actions that arise from them. Thus, bringing our own mind under control with great inner awareness and mindfulness is the way to free ourselves from suffering.

The methods for training our mind are known as meditation. Buddha taught many different levels of meditation and a variety of techniques to suit the needs or dispositions of many people. Through practicing these techniques we can achieve great tranquility and inner strength. However, our own inner tranquility is not the final goal to be achieved, but is rather a step in developing a loving attitude toward all other beings and inspiring ourselves to serve them.

Hinayana and Mahayana

So, the essence of the spiritual path (Sanskrit *dharma*) taught by Buddha lies in the development of our own inner awareness and our loving attitude toward our fellow beings. These inner qualities need to be developed stage by stage, therefore Buddha skillfully taught at different levels: the practice of the Hinayana Path, or Small Vehicle; and the practice of the Mahayana Path, or Great Vehicle. Again within the Mahayana Path there are two stages: Prajnaparamitayana, or the Path to Perfection, and Tantrayana, or the Transformational Path.

The practice of the Hinayana Path is mainly based on the development of our own inner awareness. The Mahayana Path shows very extensive methods and techniques for developing our own loving attitude toward our fellow beings and the great skills required to benefit them.

Mahayana is the complete path. All the paths that Buddha taught are included in it. It is the path of the bodhisattvas—those who seek the highest spiritual goal of enlightenment in order to be able to benefit countless living beings. Why is it called Mahayana? Here the bodhisattva Maitreya states in his commentary on the Mahayana sutras entitled *Ornament to the Mahayana Sutras*:

> The path that bodhisattvas practice is called the Great Vehicle because their motivation is great, their skill is great, their wisdom is great, their enthusiasm is great, their deeds are great, their effort is great, and their achievements are great.

The Hinayana Path and the Path to Perfection are together called Sutrayana or the Sutra Path. The essential practice in the Sutrayana is to develop our own inner awareness through the practice of the so-called three trainings: training in morality, single-pointed mind, and wisdom; and on this basis to develop an altruistic mind and great skill and knowledge to benefit our fellow beings through the practices of the six perfections: generosity, morality, patience, enthusiastic perseverance, single-pointed mind, and wisdom.

Tantrayana teaches the practice of very fine and profound techniques and skills for transforming our ordinary state of body, speech, and mind into the divine, pure state of body, speech, and mind. The practice of tantra is based on meditations on deity yoga, psychic channels, psychic nerve wheels, and energy drops within our body.

The essential practice in the Mahayana teaches meditation on the different levels of the path, ranging from Sutrayana to Tantrayana. This is known as the practice of the gradual path (Tibetan *lam rim*). In this book we present meditations on the gradual path to enlightenment based on Sutrayana.

Atisha

This system of meditations was transmitted from Buddha through his two great disciples, Maitreya and Manjushri, to the present-day teachers. This living tradition of the gradual path practice is based on the teachings of the Indian Buddhist yogi, or practitioner, Atisha (982–1054 CE) and the Tibetan Buddhist yogi and scholar, Lama Tsonghkapa (1357–1419 CE), who founded the Gelug tradition of Tibetan Buddhism (popularly known as the Yellow Hat).

Atisha was born in eastern India as the son of King Gevaipal. From his childhood Atisha was highly respected for his exceptional moral conduct and profound knowledge. One day, as a small child, whilst sleeping beside his mother, there was a loud noise from the ceiling of their room. His parents saw an incredibly beautiful bunch of blue utpala flowers fall down onto the child. But what Atisha saw was Tara, the female manifestation of Buddha's limitless activities. Thereafter, Atisha had constant visions of Tara, who always gave him guidance and teachings. As a young man he met his first guru, the yogi Master Zetari, from whom he took many teachings. From that time on Atisha studied intensively with many of the greatest

Indian yogis of the day and became renowned for his practice and knowledge of Lord Buddha's teachings on both sutra and tantra.

One day Atisha wondered, "Which is the most essential practice for achieving enlightenment quickly to be able to benefit all sentient beings?" One of his main gurus, Master Rahula, suddenly appeared in a vision. Rahula said to him, "You have great knowledge of sutra and tantra as well as profound experience of tantric meditation, yet the essence of the path by which all buddhas have achieved enlightenment is bodhicitta, the altruistic mind." Tara also told Atisha the same and asked him to go and find the guru who could give him pure instructions on how to develop this altruistic aspiration to commit oneself to attaining enlightenment.

Eventually, Atisha heard of Lama Serlingpa, or Dharmakirti, and when he heard of his great qualities he was so moved with joy that tears filled his eyes. Master Serlingpa was then meditating and teaching in a place called Ser Ling, or Golden Island, in Indonesia. Atisha decided to go at once to receive the precious teachings on bodhicitta. He traveled with many of his own disciples and arrived after a long and arduous voyage. Atisha spent twelve years with his master, receiving the precious teachings and practicing meditation on bodhicitta under his guidance. Thus, the great Atisha developed incredible experience of bodhicitta.

After returning to India, Atisha traveled to Tibet at the invitation of the Tibetan King Jangchub Ö. There he taught the meditations on bodhicitta extensively. At the request of the king he composed the exceptional text called *The Lamp of the Path to Enlightenment*, in which he systematically presents the pure, traditional practices of meditation on the gradual path passed down by Buddha, through early great Buddhist yogis, to Atisha himself.

Transmission from a Master or Guru

Traditionally, the gradual path is practiced under the guidance of a spiritual master from whom one takes a transmission (see below). Hence, it is very important to choose a qualified master with whom we feel a close, positive connection.

Buddha mentioned in his sutra and tantra teachings the qualities that a spiritual master requires. The spiritual masters who give pure teachings on the gradual path are masters of the Mahayana teachings and the qualities they require are described by Maitreya in his *Ornament to the Mahayana Sutras*:

> We should rely on those who have the following ten qualities as our spiritual masters: They are well-disciplined in pure morality, well-trained in single-pointed mind, and well-trained in wisdom. They have greater scriptural knowledge than we as disciples; they have great enthusiasm in teaching and practicing; they have great knowledge of the three vessels of Buddha's teachings—the Vinaya, Abhidharma, and Sutras; they have the realization of the ultimate truth and are expert at teaching Dharma; they have pure compassion and never tire of benefiting others.

Concerning the practitioner of the gradual path, Master Aryadeva, the chief disciple of Nagarjuna, says in his *Four Hundred-Verse Madhyamika (Middle Way)*:

> Those who have an unbiased mind and have the ability to discern the right path from the wrong, who have a sincere and genuine interest in the teachings and practice received from the spiritual master, are suitable to be disciples.

Having chosen our spiritual master, we receive transmission of the practice of the gradual path. There are three stages of transmission. At the first, the spiritual master gives a detailed commentary on the scriptures that outline the path. The disciple needs to study these scriptures—such as Atisha's *Lamp of the Path to Enlightenment* or other texts written by meditation masters on this subject—in order to become familiar with the practices on the path.

In the second transmission, the spiritual master gives an explanation of the practice from his or her personal experience. At this stage more emphasis is placed on practicing what we have learned from our spiritual master than from books.

In the third transmission, the spiritual master gives personal guidance on how to practice meditation on the path, stage by stage. At this stage we strictly follow his instructions and whenever certain problems or good experiences arise within our practice, we have to consult our kind master and do as he advises.

The Levels of the Path

The ultimate goal of practicing the Buddha's teachings is to gain complete inner purity and the fully developed realization of the truth, known as enlightenment. The reason for seeking such a state is to be able to benefit countless beings. Enlightenment is attained by eliminating our delusions through an ever deeper understanding of wisdom and the skillful means of altruism. This can only be done gradually, through practicing stage by stage, as laid out in the gradual path. Lord Buddha states in the sutra *Request by the Master of Mantra*:

> Expert jewelers purify precious gems by removing the dirt that stains them layer by layer. Through this process they produce magnificent, priceless gem ornaments. Similarly, the Enlightened Ones, seeing the presence of the obscured buddha nature in all beings, show them the doctrine of Dharma, so that they can purify their minds of delusion stage by stage. Through progression in such methods beings finally attain enlightenment.

For this reason the teachings on the path set out systematic stages of practicing meditation.

Traditionally, the practice of the path is divided into three stages: the initial, medium, and high levels. These reflect the levels of awareness to be developed by each practitioner.

The Levels of the Path in This Book

Part One explains how we prepare ourselves for the practice of the path. Part Two presents the initial level, at which we inspire ourselves to practice a spiritual path by meditating on the value of our precious human rebirth (chapter 6) and the impermanence of life (chapter 7). Then, seeing the need for guidance and protection, we meditate on taking refuge (chapter

8). These realizations open up our mind to the possibility of happiness in future lifetimes, beyond the short-term pleasures of this life alone.

At the medium level, which is presented in Part Three, we mainly contemplate the suffering nature of all our rebirths, so-called cyclic existence (Sanskrit *samsara*) (chapter 9). This helps us to seek everlasting happiness beyond the confused states of cyclic existence—the happiness that arises from fully subduing our delusions.

We are then led to the high level of practice, presented in Parts Four and Five. At first we practice extensive meditations on developing love and compassion toward all our fellow beings equally: we meditate on equanimity; on the recognition of all beings as our mother; on remembering their kindness; on exchanging ourself with others; on giving our own happiness to others and taking their suffering upon ourself (chapters 10 and 11).

Once we achieve a genuine experience of love for all beings, as if each one of them were our most beloved child, and of bodhicitta, or the altruistic mind, we enter the Bodhisattva Path, which is based on the practices of the six perfections and the four skillful means (chapter 12). The six perfections are explained in general and the first four—generosity, morality, patience, and enthusiastic perseverance—in detail (chapter 13). Meditations on the first four perfections follow this (chapter 14). The last two perfections are dealt with separately because they are so important and extensive. The fifth perfection—single-pointed mind—is introduced as the basis of the sixth (chapter 15) and we are shown extensive methods to develop the fully trained state of single-pointed mind (chapter 16) with short methods to develop some experience of it at the end of this chapter. The sixth perfection—the wisdom of emptiness—is introduced within the context of different Buddhist philosophical schools (chapter 17) and an analytical meditation on emptiness—the ultimate antidote to our delusions—is explained in detail (chapter 18).

This is the practice of Sutrayana. Once we are well-trained in this we are ready to start the practice of Tantrayana, which is, however, not the subject of this book.

Meditation

The actual method to achieve the realizations of the path is meditation. This is *gom* in Tibetan, meaning to acquaint or familiarize. What it actually means is to familiarize ourselves with higher states of mind such as positive and clear or undeluded states, compassion, a loving attitude toward others, and the clarity of wisdom. By becoming familiar with these we can gradually develop them within ourselves and eventually our mind can become fully transformed into a pure state.

There are two different kinds of meditation: single-pointed meditation and analytical meditation. To achieve realizations we need not only calmness, clarity, and stability of mind—which are the result of single-pointed meditation—but also penetrative insight—the result of analytical meditation.

Once our mind becomes calm, clear, and stable, then on the basis of this we analyze or reflect on lines of reasoning to see deeply the truth of whatever subject we meditate on. Finally, through penetration, we gain the actual experience of whatever aspect of the path we are meditating on. These experiences are called realizations. This is the actual path that leads us to our goal, be it liberation from suffering or full enlightenment.

Meditation can be applied not only to a fixed meditation session but also to all rounds of daily life. Keeping our bodily activity, speech, and thoughts in a virtuous or positive state in any situation in our daily lives is meditation, too. According to Buddha's teachings, this is how we can achieve happiness within ourselves.

When we hear about the incredible beauties of Buddhadharma we may think overwhelmingly, "This is what I should do." This is the first step—the important thing is to practice consistently and sincerely, because it is only through such practice that we can achieve our goal.

All pure spiritual paths are a means to fulfill the needs of us all—each sentient being—and therefore the fulfillment of our inner needs is the goal of all pure spiritual paths. From our own experience we require both material comfort and inner understanding. Buddhism was taught by Buddha Shakyamuni more than two thousand five hundred years ago; Buddha himself searched for, and attained, the complete path whereby true freedom from all suffering and true everlasting happiness is gained. As a result Buddha fully realized that training one's own mind is the right path; he said:

> If the mind is not trained it brings about endless suffering. If we train the mind it brings constant joy and happiness; therefore the spiritual path is nothing other than the purification of our own thoughts.

Shantideva also points out that being mindful of the actions of our mind, body, and speech is the key practice of training one's own mind. With regard to progressing along our own spiritual path, Buddha mentioned in the Sutras:

> Just as jewelers purify jewels step by step and produce pure shining jewels, so our mind needs to be trained through purification, step by step.

Buddhism therefore presents meditations on the graduated path ranging from the path of small scope through the path of the higher scope, as we present in this book.

PART ONE

Basic Requirements for the Practice of Meditation

Lama Tsonghkapa

1. The Meaning of the Gradual Path to Enlightenment (Lam Rim)

The essence of Buddhist practice lies in training our own mind so that we gradually eliminate negative states of mind and develop positive ones.

The unsubdued mind brings suffering and the subdued mind is the source of peace and happiness. When all negative thought has been completely eliminated by our developing positive states of mind, the ultimate nature of our mind is fully realized. This is what we call enlightenment.

The systematic methods for developing positive states of mind—from the practice of morality to the enlightened state—are presented in the traditional teachings known as the gradual path to enlightenment.

The origin of these teachings is the text *The Lamp of the Path to Enlightenment* written by the great Indian bodhisattva, Atisha. This text was and still is the foundation of Mahayana practice and is considered to be essential practice in all traditions of Tibetan Buddhism, as well as in the Indian Buddhist traditions. The treatise is very short but extensive in meaning, marvelously showing how to practice the whole path to enlightenment. The system it presents is based on the experience of many Buddhist yogis and is therefore very accessible and applicable.

One of the significant points of the teachings on the path is that they show us clearly how to practice and directly apply to our daily lives any Dharma or spiritual knowledge we may gain. Through the practice of great awareness and mindfulness, for example, we can relate the experience we gain during a meditation session to our everyday life.

The teachings on the path are considered to be the key to utilizing the teachings of all the sutras and tantras taught by Lord Buddha Shakyamuni. By clearly understanding this system we will know how to take whatever we learn into our practice systematically. For example, whenever we hear teachings about suffering, or compassion. or any other virtuous topic, we can immediately understand how to cultivate them in our minds and practice them. So these teachings are practical and effective.

Not only do they show the methods for gaining realizations in meditation sessions, they also show us how to conduct our body, speech, and mind in a positive way. This enables us to maintain a peaceful atmosphere within ourselves, and outwardly toward the people we meet in our daily lives. If we sincerely integrate the instructions on the path into our daily activities, even when we are cleaning our home or doing our job, everything we do becomes more valuable and meaningful to us.

These teachings always guide us on how to deal positively with any difficulties or problems that may arise in our daily lives. For example, when we have to face criticism, hostility, or deception, they show us how to develop the strength of patience, or how to develop compassion and love toward people around us through our experience of our own suffering and difficulties. And when we lose something to which we are very attached, they clearly show us how to counter disappointment and depression. In brief, they reveal how to use any unfortunate situation to develop our inner understanding and strength.

In Drepung Monastery, one of the largest monastic universities in Tibet, there was once a practitioner named Kyarpon Rinpoche. He is considered by many to be as great as Milarepa, the well-known yogi who lived in Tibet at the end of the eleventh century. Kyarpon left the monastery and spent more than thirty years alone in a cave, living on very poor-quality food, mostly wild plants. In the winter time it was extremely cold high up in the mountains, yet Kyarpon remained living in the cave without warm food or warm clothing. In spite of the harsh conditions, he was always found to be happy and smiling. When people went to visit him they were surprised at this and asked him, "How can you be so happy, living in such poor conditions?" Rinpoche replied, "With the help of the teachings on the gradual path, I understand a little about the nature of samsaric life. Maybe because of this…" and he began to laugh.

We can see how useful these teachings are! All experienced yogis equally hold this system in high esteem. It enables us to make our present life happier and, at the same time, helps us to plant seeds on our mindstream that will produce wholesome fruit in our future lives. Thus, the teachings of Lord Buddha lead us from happy states to happy results.

We may wonder what it means to practice these teachings. Is it something to do with reciting mantras or holy words, living in a temple, making offerings, or sitting in the meditation posture? From the point of view of Buddha's teachings, Dharma, or spiritual practice, is not separate from our daily activities. It is nothing other than virtuous actions of body, speech, and mind because this is what really protects us and others from suffering. If, for instance, when talking to people we have a respectful and compassionate attitude toward them, our speech itself becomes Dharma, no matter what we talk about. Or if we work with a sincere attitude, the action itself becomes Dharma, whatever job we do. As a virtuous mind leads to wholesome actions and a deluded mind leads to non-virtuous actions, it is essential to train our mind in virtuous thought.

There are five aspects of virtue. Although the mind is not virtuous by nature, when associated with virtuous mental states it becomes virtuous; this is technically known as being virtuous by (1) *being associated with virtuous mental states.*

The mind and mental states are different: the mind flows continuously and mental states, although part of the mind, arise temporarily and then cease. There are different kinds of mental states: virtuous, non-virtuous, and neutral. Some of the virtuous states are clarity, calmness, patience, and love. These mental states are virtuous from the beginning and are therefore called (2) *virtues by nature.*

When these virtuous states arise they always lead to constructive speech and actions, therefore whether what we say and do becomes virtuous, non-virtuous, or neutral depends on our mind. Constructive actions are called (3) *virtues by motivation.*

Our virtuous mental states not only lead to constructive actions, they also plant positive seeds on our consciousness for future wholesome results; these potentials are called (4) *seedling virtues.*

As we develop pure actions of mind, speech, and body, deluded states of mind decrease and eventually disappear altogether. This is called (5) *ultimate virtue* because it is the highest virtue, completely free from all non-virtuous states. It is the complete freedom from the suffering of cyclic existence (Sanskrit *nirvana*).

With the help of the teachings on the gradual path we can develop these virtues. However, it is not sufficient merely to have the instructions on the path. They have to be put into practice and this depends entirely on ourselves—how sincere we are in our practice.

Rebirth and the Nature of the Mind

Our virtuous and non-virtuous actions performed through mind, speech, and body sow seeds on our consciousness for future fruits. Depending on our circumstances and whether conditions are conducive or not, these seeds can ripen in this life or in future lifetimes. Our mind, or consciousness, goes unceasingly from one life to the next.

The nature of our mind is different from that of our body. Unlike our body, our mind is not a genetic product which developed biologically from the parental sperm and ovum cells. Every part of our body, from the limbs to the cells, is something that is physiologically composed of atoms and sub-atomic particles. However, mind has a totally different nature. It has no physical characteristics as our body does. It is completely formless, yet has a clear nature that can reflect any object. Therefore, mind is not the same as the brain, it is something beyond the physical state. It is a continuous flow, changing moment by moment. For instance, the state of mind of this very moment arises from the immediately preceding moment of consciousness; the previous one arose from its immediately preceding moment of consciousness and so on.

As consciousness arises only from the preceding moment of consciousness, the first moment of the embryo's mind is not developed from the two parental biological cells, as its body is. It comes from its preceding moment of consciousness in the so-called intermediate state between this life and the previous one. And in turn, the consciousness of the intermediate state comes from the previous rebirth. At the time of conception, when the sperm cell of the father unites with and fertilizes the ovum in the mother's womb, our previous consciousness—which existed in the intermediate state—enters into the fertilized cell. This is one kind of rebirth.

There are three other kinds of rebirth: rebirth in an egg-shell, in moisture, and through miraculous power. Whatever kind of rebirth we take, our consciousness enters into the new body at the time of conception.

Consciousness always flows with a stream of subtle energy, the so-called subtle psychic winds (Sanskrit *prana*). Consciousness and the subtle psychic winds are inseparable. At the time of conception this subtle wind energy moves from the previous life to the fertilized ovum, taking the previous consciousness with it. Similarly, at the time of death, the subtle wind energy leaves this body and moves to the next life, taking the consciousness with it. This is how consciousness moves from one life to another.

When consciousness enters into the fertilized egg, the subtle wind energy takes this new body as its home and resides in it. Thus, consciousness remains within the body until the time of death. Our consciousness and subtle psychic wind energy abide in the core of the fertilized ovum. As the new body develops, the psychic winds gradually become active to form subtle psychic nerves or channels (Sanskrit *nadi*) in the embryo's body and psychic nerve wheels (Sanskrit *chakras*) are gradually formed. When the embryo reaches the state where its body is developed into the human form, the formation of the psychic channels and chakras is complete.

There are three main psychic channels (see illustration on page 188), which are important for the circulation of wind energy. All three are located within the embryo's body from the head down to the sex organ. They start between the eyebrows, go up to the crown of the head just inside the skull where they bend and go straight down to the sex organ, keeping close to the spinal cord. They are of a very fine and luminous nature. The central channel has six main chakras: between the eyebrows, just below the crown of the head, and at the level of the throat, heart, navel, and sex organ. Inside the heart chakra there is a psychic energy drop (Sanskrit *bindhu*) which is composed of the white and red energy drops: the white energy drop is the subtle essential energy that comes from the father and the red one is subtle energy that comes from the mother. This is the place where our subtle consciousness and subtle wind energy remain until we die. From this subtle wind energy grows the gross wind energy, which flows through the spokes of the chakras to the different parts of our body. At the same time as the gross wind energy arises from the subtle wind energy, the gross conceptual and sensory consciousness also grows from the subtle consciousness. When this happens we experience external objects through our senses and our consciousness becomes involved in thinking about what we experience.

At the time of death the power of the elements within the body gradually decreases and dissolves into the subtle psychic wind energy. First the earth element dissolves into the water element; then the water element dissolves into the heat element; the heat element dissolves into gross wind energy and this in turn finally dissolves into the subtle wind energy that is inseparably united with the subtle consciousness inside the central channel at the heart level. At the same time our gross sensory and conceptual consciousness dissolves into the subtle consciousness; therefore, for a while we do not have any gross conceptual memory and sensation, but we do experience certain inner visions. The subtle consciousness flows on continuously. It is this consciousness that moves from this life to the next at the last moment of death.

As soon as our subtle consciousness leaves this body together with the subtle wind energy, gross wind energy arises again from the subtle one to form the body of the intermediate state. This body is very subtle, like a dream experience. Our consciousness will remain in this state until it meets the right circumstances or conditions for its next rebirth. When it finds these it enters into the new body.

The Law of Cause and Effect

In this way our consciousness moves unceasingly from one life to another. What impels this cycle of existence is, in fact, our own desire and attachment, as well as all our other deluded states of mind. There is, then, a link between our life now, our previous ones, and our future lives: whatever we do, think, and say creates seeds, or imprints, which remain on our stream of consciousness to ripen when the right conditions come together. Just as seeds need soil, water, and heat to ripen, so do the seeds on our mindstream need the right external conditions as well as the internal ones of desire and attachment; without these, they cannot ripen.

When the right conditions do come together we experience the results of our past actions. This is called *karma,* or the law of cause and effect. Buddha says:

Negative states of mind such as anger, hatred, jealousy, or pride lead us to say and do negative things. These actions bring us undesirable results in the future. Positive states of mind lead us to positive actions of body and speech, which bring us desirable or happy results.

Therefore, our future is dependent on our present actions.

However, do not think that there is no hope and that just because we have done bad actions in the past we deserve to suffer and can do nothing about it. The point is that we *can* abandon our suffering and improve our conditions. If we stop doing negative actions and develop virtuous mind, virtuous speech, and virtuous actions, we can purify all our past negativities. Hence it becomes essential to discipline or train our mind, body, and speech in virtue. This is the practice of Dharma as taught by Buddha.

Through disciplining our mind, body, and speech we can achieve a stable and clear state of mind, whereby we can gain the realization of the ultimate truth. This truth leads us to complete freedom from all delusions and the resultant suffering.

2. The Four Significant Qualities
of the Gradual Path

Atisha's main disciple, Dromön Rinpoche, said:

> I cannot see that there is a single word among Buddha's teachings
> that is not meant for training our minds.

The path to enlightenment is a most instructive method, showing us how
to practice all Buddha's teachings stage by stage in the most effective way.
The great master Tsonghkapa points out the significance of the four unique
qualities of the path thus:

1 The gradual path shows us the method of how to take all
   Buddha's teachings into our practice without seeing any contra-
   diction in them. For example, in the lower stage of Vinaya practice, the practice of discipline, Buddha rejected possessing
   precious material things. However, at the higher stage of bodhisattva practice, they are allowed, because there is no danger of
   increasing our desire; they can be used for the benefit of other
   beings.

2 The teachings on the path enable us to see all Buddha's teachings in an unbiased way and to take them as personal instructions for training and subduing our own mind.

3 Having understood these two points, we will clearly see the ultimate intention of Lord Buddha, which is to lead us to buddhahood by giving many different teachings according to the
   progress of our understanding.

4 Since the gradual path presents a sound system that enables us
   to incorporate all levels of Buddha's teachings into this single
   method of training our own mind, we will never fall under the
   influence of any kind of sectarian view.

3. Our Motivation for Practicing Meditation

Motivation plays a very important role in our Dharma practice. Whether it becomes fruitful or not is determined by our motivation; therefore, all yogis place much more emphasis on generating pure motivation than on meditating on the actual path itself. Lama Tsonghkapa says:

> Whether our practice becomes Mahayana, leading to the enlightened state, or Hinayana, leading only to self-liberation, does not depend on which path we practice, but on what attitude motivates us to practice.

The First Panchen Lama wrote a book in which he answers many important questions relating to practical meditation. On being asked how we should begin meditation on the gradual path, he answered, "Whatever path we meditate on, we should begin by checking our mental attitude." Similarly, Geshe Chen Ngawa, a Kadampa lama, or follower of Atisha's teachings, says:

> Whenever we do any spiritual practice, we should check our motivation at the beginning and generate pure dedication at the end. These two activities are very important.

Therefore, whatever Dharma practice we do, whether it is listening to teachings, reading or reciting scriptures, meditating, or giving teachings, it is essential to try to correct our attitude at the beginning and not forget to generate pure dedication at the end.

The Three Defective Attitudes

Regarding our motivation for listening to the Dharma, there are three defective attitudes to be abandoned.

The first is likened to a pot being kept upside down. This pot cannot hold anything, implying a lack of attention on the part of the listener. For instance, people may come to a discourse yet not bother to pay attention to what is being discussed. So, despite their physical presence, they cannot gain much understanding from the teaching. Or suppose someone were to offer you a precious medicinal liquid; if you hold out the pot, upside down, you will not be able to receive it.

The second defect in our attitude to listening to Dharma is likened to a cracked vessel. If you keep the medicinal liquid in a cracked container, the precious liquid will gradually drain away, leaving not a drop when you wish to drink it. This implies a lack of mindfulness. Even though we may pay good attention during a discourse, if we do not bother to maintain what we have heard with mindfulness, we will not have much understanding when we practice later on. It is very important to develop our memory by constantly reminding ourselves of whatever insights we have gained from listening to teachings, or from our own experience resulting from our practice. For this purpose we practice a particular method of meditation called *shar gom* in Tibetan. *Shar* means to clarify within the mind the subject matter we are going to meditate on, and *gom*, as mentioned, means to be familiar with the subject of meditation. In other words, we reflect again and again on the Dharma subjects we have learned.

The third defective attitude is likened to a pot that is stained with dirt. If we keep the medicinal liquid in a dirty pot, it will become spoiled. Similarly, although we receive very pure teachings coming from the heart of the most compassionate Buddha, if we listen and then practice with an impure motivation, our practice will become stained. Motivation is so important!

There have been many cases of tantric practitioners who practiced with the incorrect motivation of harming others through magic power. As a result of this bad motivation, after they died, they fell into a rebirth in the realm of hungry ghosts (Sanskrit *preta*), one of the three lower realms.

Needless to say, to practice Buddhist tantra we need to generate the pure motivation of bodhicitta. Without this, no matter how much tantra we practice or how much effort we make in meditation, we will not be able to gain any realizations.

When Atisha was living in India in a monastery called Otantaputra, there was a tantric practitioner who had been meditating on Hevajra yoga with great effort for many years. This is one of the highest tantras, but his motivation was to liberate himself from suffering in cyclic existence. As a result of practicing this tantra for so long, he had reached certain levels of realization. But he himself was not sure which level he had reached, so he went to ask Atisha. Atisha discovered that he had entered the Hinayana Path through practicing tantric methods, but because of his motivation had only gained the level of Stream-Enterer, the lower goal in the Sravaka Path.

Some disciples of Atisha asked him how they should distinguish what is Dharma from non-Dharma. Atisha replied, "From your motivation. If you practice tantra with any of the eight wordly motivations, the practice cannot even be the lowest Dharma." Then they asked Atisha, "If the highest Dharma is practiced with a bad motivation, what result is gained?" He answered, "Nothing else but rebirth in hell, in the preta realm or in the miserable animal realm." Therefore, when Kadampa lamas engage in any spiritual practice, they always check whether their minds are influenced by any of the eight worldly attitudes.

The Eight Worldly Attitudes

1 Desire for fame.
2 Feeling unhappy or anguished when we lose fame.
3 Desire for worldly pleasure.
4 Feeling unhappy when we lose worldly pleasure.
5 Desire for material gain.
6 Feeling unhappy when we lose material gain.
7 Desire for praise.
8 Feeling anguished when we hear harsh or unpleasant words toward ourselves.

These eight attitudes are called the "eight inner evils" by the Kadampa lamas, because they always make us unhappy and cause us to harm others as well. As long as our mind is dominated by any one of these, we can hardly rest in true peace and happiness, despite material comforts.

There is always the danger of being deluded by these attitudes when we practice Dharma, unless we have reached the level where desire for pleasure within this life is overcome. Kadampa lamas always try to take the blame upon themselves, in order to get rid of pride over their qualities or desire for fame.

Once there was a great Kadampa lama called Ben Gonggyal, who used to be a robber. He met Dromtön Rinpoche and after receiving the bodhicitta teachings from him he meditated only on bodhicitta for the rest of his life. One day he was invited by a rich family to spend a few days with them. While he was there, he found himself taking some tea from the teapot without asking them. Suddenly he shouted, "Great yogi is now stealing things!"

His Holiness the Dalai Lama always warns us about using Dharma for the wrong reason:

> According to Lord Buddha's teaching, the cause of suffering is delusion, particularly unsubdued desire. The only antidote to desire and delusion is Dharma practice. If we use the Dharma with the desire for fame and so on, rather than for overcoming desire, then there would be no method left to abandon delusion. This is likened to fire breaking out and water being the only way to extinguish it. If water becomes fire, there is no other way to extinguish fire. Therefore, if you sincerely want to practice Dharma, practice purely!

For instance, Marpa, who was the founder of the Kagyu tradition of Tibetan Buddhism, achieved extremely high realizations on the tantric level, yet always considered himself lower, just like ordinary people. He was never arrogant, but always behaved as a simple farmer. Nowadays we paint him depicted on a high throne with many ornaments, but in fact he was not like that. He worked in the fields.

The Dharma that most of us are practicing is the highest, but what is our motivation? We are discussing the Mahayana, or bodhisattva, teachings, which are incredibly beautiful and beneficial, so if we practice them with good motivation, there is no doubt that we shall gain many benefits.

But if we do not subdue our own pride and the desire for our own selfish gain within this life, it is quite difficult to generate the Mahayana motivation, the attitude wishing purely to benefit others. So it is better to consider ourself lower and to develop respect for others. Many experienced practitioners stress that this kind of attitude really helps us to overcome our selfishness, which always makes us irritable and unhappy.

You may wonder how, if you give up your own happiness and become concerned only with the happiness of others, you can survive or achieve your own happiness. The great eighth century bodhisattva Shantideva says:

> It is the self-cherishing mind that always causes us endless suffering. Therefore, when we neglect ourselves and consider others to be more important, we automatically become happier and happier, because we are not so anxious about our own prosperity and do not have much desire.

Therefore, it is essential to check our motivation and if we find any of the three defective attitudes, or the eight worldly motivations, we should try to abandon them.

The Six Positive Attitudes

Regarding our motivation for listening to the Dharma, there are six positive attitudes to be taken up. These are:

1 To consider ourselves as patients in the sense that we are suffering from delusion.
2 To consider the Dharma as being the perfect medicine.
3 To consider the teacher who administers the Dharma, which comes purely from Lord Buddha, as the physician.
4 To become confident in the fact that we will be completely cured of our sickness by practicing Dharma.
5 To develop great faith in Buddha as being the perfect guide who can lead us completely beyond suffering.
6 To develop the great wish that Buddha's precious teachings may live long, fulfilling the needs of countless beings.

Even though we all constantly thirst after happiness and hate having even a little suffering, we have no understanding of the root of our suffering or of the true path to achieving everlasting happiness. Therefore, whenever we face an unhappy situation or hardship of any kind, we ignorantly put the blame on others and often even hate ourselves; thus we experience endless suffering.

However, the root of all the suffering that we experience in this life is nothing other than untamed thoughts within our own mind. If we truly wish to liberate ourselves from suffering, we should try to recognize the truth that our own deluded thoughts are the cause of all suffering and should sincerely seek the true methods for subduing them. Maitreya Buddha says:

> Sick people will first try to recognize the root of their disease and, having discovered it, will seek the appropriate medicine; as a result they will gradually regain the happiness of their health. In the same way, those who wish for freedom from the endless suffering of samsara should first of all analyze what is the true root of their suffering. Having understood it, they should undertake the practice of whatever is appropriate for removing the root of their own suffering. Through sincerely practicing such methods, they will be able to gain total freedom from the suffering of samsara.

In this sense the Buddhadharma is the true medicine for us. It can cure us of our endless suffering because it shows us how to subdue our deluded minds, using very profound and effective methods based on systematic stages and logical reasoning.

4. The Levels of the Path

There are three successive stages of meditation on the path, which correspond to our progressing levels of realization or inner awareness.

At the initial level we are shown how to be aware of our own gross sufferings and we are also shown the right method to deal with them. This method embodies meditation on the impermanence of this present life and the sufferings of beings born in any of the three lower realms: the animal realm, the hungry ghost realm, and the hell realms. This practice leads us to develop virtuous moral conduct, through which we continue to gain a happy rebirth in a higher realm. Another higher rebirth ensures that we can continue our Dharma practice in future lives.

At the medium level the main emphasis is placed on awareness of the sufferings of beings in the whole of cyclic existence, which includes the three higher realms: the human, demi-god, and god realms. We need to see the suffering of others in order to be able to develop great love and compassion. But we cannot deeply see the suffering in others without being fully aware of our own sufferings, first at the gross level, then at the subtle. Therefore, meditation on our own subtle suffering serves as a ground for generating great compassion at the third stage. When we gain the realization of the suffering nature of the whole of cyclic existence, we are able to develop morality, single-pointed mind, and wisdom. As a result of this, from this stage onward we are able to subdue our own undisciplined mind and therefore achieve great mental stability and tranquility.

At the third stage we extend our understanding toward all other beings and thus inspire ourselves to attain enlightenment for their sake. Not only do we free ourselves from suffering, but we are able to benefit others to be free from the suffering of cyclic existence.

It is very important to practice the path stage by stage as laid out in the scriptures, because each stage serves as a foundation for gaining realizations on the next. The Buddha explained this with an analogy of how jewelers purify precious stones in the sutra called *Request by the Master of Mantra*:

O son or daughter of noble family, take the example of jewelers who have great skill and expertise in polishing gemstones. Upon seeing a soiled gemstone, they take it and clean it in acrid, salt water. Having done that they then polish it with a hair-cloth. However, they do not stop their effort after the first attempt, they then clean it in a strong acidic solution and polish it better with a woollen cloth. Having done that, even then they do not relent in their effort; they clean it in a medicinal liquid and polish it with a very fine cloth. Thus, they completely clean the gemstone and transform it into the most precious piece of lapis lazuli.

O son or daughter of noble family, in the same way Enlightened Ones, having seen our buddha nature being obscured by delusion, lead us to realize the suffering nature of cyclic existence through teachings on impermanence and the suffering nature of the whole of cyclic existence. In this way they inspire us in the practice of morality.

The Enlightened Ones do not give up their effort. Having done that, they then lead us further to the realization of selflessness, signlessness, and desirelessness. Through this we are guided to see the tathagata essence.

Again at this stage the Enlightened Ones do not stop their approach. They inspire us to enter into the realm of the Tathagata [Buddha] by expounding the doctrines of the irreversible vehicle and also the voidness of the inherent existence of the three circles, relating to subject, object, and action.

Thus, Enlightened Ones fully lead us to complete purification of the defilements that obscure our buddha nature, which is everpresent within us.

In this extract Buddha clearly mentions how to achieve enlightenment by purifying our mind of delusions through three stages with the analogy of how expert jewelers cleanse precious stones, layer by layer.

The first stage is the stage of developing the realization of impermanence and the suffering nature of cyclic existence. Within this stage there are two sub-stages: the first is realizing the impermanence of this life and the suffering nature of the lower realms. This corresponds to the initial level in the practice of the gradual path. The second sub-stage is that of developing the realization of impermanence and the suffering nature of the whole of cyclic existence. This corresponds to the medium level. Thus, at the first stage mentioned in this quotation we develop our own inner awareness and subdue our gross delusions.

At the second stage the realization of the ultimate truth is developed. In this quotation the ultimate truth is mentioned in terms of selflessness, signlessness, and desirelessness. Selflessness refers to the emptiness of present phenomena. Signlessness indicates the emptiness of past phenomena. And desirelessness reveals the emptiness of phenomena to come in the future. Realizing the emptiness of these three phenomena is the ultimate antidote to our own delusions. When all our delusions, together with their subtle imprints, are completely eliminated, the pure essence of our mind is fully manifest. This is what is known as enlightenment—the goal that bodhisattvas seek for the sake of other sentient beings.

To achieve enlightenment, it is not sufficient to develop ultimate wisdom alone, we also need to develop the great loving mind equally toward all fellow beings and the great skill and ability to fulfill their needs. The third stage is where we develop this altruistic mind and great skill. In this quotation it is called the stage of practicing the irreversible vehicle, so called because this practice—the union of ultimate wisdom and the altruistic mind—directly leads us to the attainment of enlightenment, without falling back to the two extremes of rebirth within cyclic existence or of resting in mere liberation for our own peace. The last two stages—developing ultimate wisdom and altruism—correspond to the practice of meditation on bodhicitta and the practices of the Bodhisattva Path, or the six perfections.

It is not only necessary but also very important to follow the three levels sequentially. To explain this point further: The objective of the practice of the path is to cultivate bodhicitta. Bodhicitta is not only the most sympathetic attitude in which we sacrifice our own happiness in order to attain enlightenment for the sake of all other sentient beings, but also the most fruitful. This precious, selfless altruistic mind can only arise when we have such great compassion toward all beings that we cannot bear to see them suffer endlessly in cyclic existence. Tsonghkapa says:

> No matter how much effort we make in meditating on bodhicitta, without great compassion the meditation will remain as mere words.

And the great master, Nagarjuna, says in his *Precious Garland*:

> If we truly wish to attain enlightenment for the sake of all beings, we should strive to generate unshakable bodhicitta. If we closely check up on how and from where such a precious mind arises, we will see that it comes from nowhere else but from great compassion.

As Nagarjuna says, the root of bodhicitta is great compassion. How do we develop such great compassion for others? Compassion is the sympathetic attitude, wholeheartedly caring for others and wishing to liberate them from unbearable suffering. To develop such an attitude, we first need to be able to see deeply how they suffer in cyclic existence. But we cannot truly be concerned about the suffering nature of others without first understanding our own suffering nature. Shantideva says:

> How can it be possible to develop the sense of great care for others, wishing to liberate them from cyclic existence, if we never have such a caring experience for ourself, even in our dreams?

Therefore, in the first two stages we are encouraged to develop the realization of our own suffering, which provides us with a firm foundation for generating compassion. The great Tsonghkapa says:

> When we are being encouraged to meditate on our own suffering during the first two levels, we are not being directed toward something else, but to developing bodhicitta. So it is very important to

remind ourselves of this fact every time we engage in meditation on these two levels. When we are meditating on the impermanent nature of our own life, or on cyclic existence, or whatever else we meditate on, we are approaching bodhicitta.

From this we can clearly see that the meditation on the first two stages focuses all our energies on cultivating great compassion. When we develop this, we are able to achieve many higher realizations of the Mahayana Path. Buddha Shakyamuni often reminds us in many sutras:

Only great compassion is such a powerful virtue that if we generate it, we can achieve all aspects of the Dharma automatically.

Similarly, one of Nagarjuna's main disciples, Chandrakirti, states:

When we first generate bodhicitta, compassion is as important as the seed is to the growth of the crop. During the course of our practice of the Mahayana Path, when developing realizations, compassion is as important as water in the soil is for the ripening crop. Finally, when enlightenment is attained, fulfilling the needs of all beings, compassion is likened to the fully ripened crop.

Thus, we can clearly see how the initial level serves as the ground for developing realizations that are to be gained at the medium level; and how the medium level provides us with the base upon which we can develop great compassion and the mind of enlightenment, which is the essence of the practice at the third stage.

5. Preparing Ourselves for the Actual Meditation: The Six Preliminary Practices

How to Start Meditating

It is best to practice the meditations on the path on a daily basis, so we should set up a schedule.

The early morning before sunrise is the best time for the practice of meditation, if you can manage to do so. Otherwise you can practice at any time that is convenient, with the exception of four specific times: sunrise, midday, sunset, and midnight. Yogis have experienced these as being harmful to their concentration, therefore they call these four periods "damagers or destroyers of single-pointed mind."

You can do two or even more sessions a day but it is advisable to take it easy in the beginning. Even if you feel enthusiastic, just start with one or two sessions a day and then, as your meditation improves, you can do more. You should reserve certain times every day for your practice of meditation and carry out your schedule as planned. At first keep the sessions to thirty or forty minutes and then make them longer.

You can also go on retreat, that is, practice in solitude for a certain period of time, say a week or two. We should devote our time solely to practicing meditation during this fixed period, cutting ourselves off from other activities. In retreat it is good to do four sessions a day of about two hours each.

We should proceed sequentially through the meditations as they are laid out. The traditional way to practice is to meditate on one aspect of the path until we gain at least some realization of that particular subject. Only then do we move on to the next stage. However, there is another method, which is particularly convenient if we lead a busy life: we can take a different aspect of meditation each day or every two days. For example, we can meditate on the precious human rebirth on Sunday and Monday, on impermanence on Tuesday and Wednesday, and so on. In this way we are able to cover the whole of the meditations on the gradual path briefly within two or three weeks.

Meditation means familiarizing our mind with whatever aspect of the path we are practicing. Through becoming familiar with the object of meditation, we can eventually transform our mind into the fully developed state of mind. This is how we cultivate realizations of the higher path within ourselves. Maitreya says in *The Ornament for Clear Realizations*:

> To acquaint our mind continually with the virtuous path and to examine and analyze virtuous objects *is* the path of meditation.

Whether we practice on a daily basis or in retreat, we should begin each session with the preparatory practices as explained below. Only then do we proceed with the actual meditation on the path.

The Six Preliminary Practices

The preliminary practices include all the activities we need to perform before starting any meditation. With regard to this practice there are different traditions and we follow Atisha's, which is said to have come from his main guru, Lama Serlingpa. In this tradition there are six preliminary practices:

1 Cleaning our place of meditation and displaying the objects of inspiration.
2 Arranging pure offerings.
3 Sitting in the meditation posture, taking refuge in the Three Jewels, and generating the pure thought of bodhicitta.
4 Visualizing the merit field in front of which we perform the practices of purification and accumulation of merit or positive energy.
5 Performing the Seven Limb Prayer, which contains the purification of our negative actions and the accumulation of great merit, and offering a mandala.

6   Requesting the merit field to bestow the power of their blessings upon our mind, so that we gain realizations of the path we are meditating on.

The first two practices are normally done before the first session in the morning, but can be done at the beginning of each session during retreat. The other preparatory practices are done before each session.

1. Cleaning our Place of Meditation and Displaying the Objects of Inspiration

Cleaning the place where we are going to meditate is very important, because it makes our mind joyful. In many sutras Buddha mentions five different benefits of doing this. They are: making our mind joyful; giving great joy to the minds of others; pleasing the gods and goddesses who can protect us from hindrances to our Dharma practice; accumulating virtuous karma for taking rebirth in a pure land; and beautifying the external and internal world.

When we clean the meditation area it is useful to think that we are not only cleaning the external environment but are also sweeping away our internal impure dust—our delusions–with great wisdom. Having such an attitude helps us purify our negative actions. We can also recite the following verses, reflecting on their meaning:

This dust is not only external dust, but my attachment.
This dust is not only external dust, but my hatred.
This dust is not only external dust, but my ignorance.
I shall cleanse my mind by sweeping away these three internal
    dusts.

These verses were composed by a great arhat named Arya Lamchung. It is said that he obtained arhathood, self-liberation from suffering, by reciting these verses while he was cleaning the temple where many monks and nuns practiced meditation. He was born into a Brahmin family in India at the time of Buddha. Lamchung was born with a poor memory and he found it difficult to learn anything. When he grew up he was sent to a school to learn how to read and write. In early Brahmin traditions first of all they teach two words to be memorized: *sing* and *darm*. When Lamchung tried to recite *sing*, he forgot *darm*. When he tried to recite *darm*, he forgot *sing*! His Brahmin master could not help him to learn anything, so he was sent away from school. His mother then decided to send him to the Buddhist temple where his elder brother had already become an arhat. Lamchung went to learn meditation from him, but his brother could not help him, so he was expelled from the temple.

Full of sorrow, Lamchung left the temple. As he was walking away he met Buddha, who immediately saw that he had great potential regardless of his present poor memory. He advised him to go back and clean the temple thoroughly every day. One day, while Lamchung was cleaning, the thought suddenly came to his mind, "When Buddha asked me to clean the temple, he did not mean me to clean the external dust only, but the internal dust, my delusion." And he began to recite the verses mentioned above. Whenever he cleaned the temple, he would reflect on the meaning of these words. Soon he was able to purify all his negative actions and as a result he instantly remembered all the teachings he had been unable to understand before, and attained arhathood.

After we have cleaned the area where we meditate, we should display on the shrine the objects of inspiration: statues and pictures of our guru, Buddha, and bodhisattvas. These represent not only the physical state of Enlightened Beings, but also their great attainments. Therefore, they are shining examples to us and inspire us to practice Dharma.

2. Arranging Pure Offerings

Having displayed the statues or pictures of the Buddha or bodhisattvas on the altar, we should then arrange offerings in front of them. Traditionally, there are eight different types of offering: water for drinking, water for bathing, flowers for delighting the eyes, incense for delighting the nose, light, perfume for anointing the body, food, and music.

Offering does not mean mainly to worship the Buddha and bodhisattvas; more importantly, it represents the purity of our devotion toward our Dharma practice. The Kadampa lamas say:

Offering is called *puja* in Sanskrit and means "to please." If we make beautiful offerings to the Buddha and bodhisattvas, but do so with an impure attitude, then it would not please them. They are not interested in gaining material things from us, but are pleased only when we sincerely follow the Dharma instructions they give to us. Therefore, no matter how small our material offerings are, as long as we practice sincerely, there is no greater offering to them than this.

The great Indian tantric yogi, Tilopa, said to his disciple, the great Naropa:

Although you have nothing to offer me in terms of material things, I can never receive any greater offering than your sincere practice of compassion.

Lord Buddha often says in the *Perfection Sutras*:

The greatest offerings to Buddha are the practices of skillful means and wisdom. All buddhas will be delighted with those who practice them, will hold them as their private spiritual Son or Daughter and always look after them with great care.

Therefore, whenever we engage in any offering activity, we should remember what offering means.

3. Sitting in the Meditation Posture, Taking Refuge in the Three Jewels, and Generating Bodhicitta

Regarding our physical posture for meditation, there are seven aspects of the posture that we should maintain. These are: crossing the legs into the lotus position; keeping the body upright; keeping the shoulders straight and level, without any tension; keeping the hands in the meditation posture; pointing the eyes toward the tip of the nose in a relaxed way; keeping the mouth in a normal position without being tightly closed or loosely open; keeping the tongue against the palate.

We may think that sitting in this posture is not important and so not pay much attention to it. However, this posture helps to balance our physical energy, so that when we meditate there is no tension or physical heaviness. When the energies in the body are balanced, it is much easier for us to calm our mind and make it stable. Mind is dependent on physical energies and when these are not balanced, they can easily affect the mind. Therefore, experienced yogis pay attention to their posture when they practice meditation and we should do likewise. The Kadampa lamas also praised this physical yoga.

Before we begin the contemplation of taking refuge and generating bodhicitta, we should check whether there is any mental hindrance to the meditation. Lama Tsonghkapa says, "We should not rush into meditation without checking our state of mind, otherwise, despite all our efforts, we will not be able to gain any experience."

Whatever hindrances to our meditation we face, there are many choices of antidotes to counteract them. The two major hindrances we often encounter are dullness and discursive thought. The teachings on the path urge us to take up the appropriate antidotes whenever necessary. We shall discuss both these hindrances in detail in the chapter on developing single-pointed mind, page 173 onward. For the moment we shall briefly explain some antidotes to these two major hindrances to meditation.

When our mind is not still, due to the influence of discursive thought, we should meditate on breathing. This is very effective for calming the mind.

When we find that our mind has become dull, we should either reflect on the qualities of Buddha and the higher bodhisattvas, or visualize a pinpoint of light in between our eyebrows. This kind of meditation can help to elevate our mind, bring joy to it and also refresh it.

Once our mind is still and clear, we are ready to contemplate taking refuge and to generate bodhicitta. We should think like this:

It is extremely sad to see how much suffering all beings, including myself, have experienced through countless rebirths in cyclic existence since beginningless time. Unless I am able to do something about it, we shall experience endless suffering in the future as well. I am so fortunate to have found this perfect human rebirth, which enables me to attain even the enlightened state within one lifetime. Yet if I waste it, it will be extremely difficult to obtain such a precious human rebirth again. There is nothing of greater importance to me, therefore, than to try to attain enlightenment, not only for myself but also for the sake of all sentient begins. At the moment, however, I have no power to help even a few beings to be liberated from the suffering of samsara. Who can help me to fulfill my wish to liberate all beings from suffering? Only the Three Jewels have such power. Therefore I take refuge in the Jewel of Buddha, the Jewel of Dharma, and the Jewel of Sangha (see page 73). I shall attain enlightenment at any cost so that I may liberate all my mother sentient beings from the unbearable sufferings of samsara.

Having contemplated in this way, we should recite the following verse three times:

> I go for refuge until I am enlightened
> To the buddhas, the Dharma, and the Highest Assembly.
> From the virtuous merit that I collect
> By practicing giving and other perfections,
> May I attain the state of a buddha
> To be able to benefit all sentient beings.

4. Visualizing the Merit Field

We now visualize the merit field, meaning the buddhas, bodhisattvas, and so on, who inspire us in our practice. Visualize in front of you a large wish-fulfilling tree arising from the middle of a calm and beautiful white lake of nectar. On the tree is a large, golden throne supported by eight snow lions; on the throne is a beautiful lotus. On the lotus is a sun disc and on top of that a moon disc, both of which are cushions of light. In the middle of the moon disc, on a smaller golden throne, is seated Lord Buddha Shakyamuni, who is inseparably one with the guru from whom you mainly receive the teachings of this practice, the gradual path.

Encircling Buddha Shakyamuni are first your other gurus; then the tantric deities; then the other buddhas and bodhisattvas; the Pratyeka buddhas and Sravaka arhats (Hinayana practitioners); dakas and dakinis (highly realized tantric yogis); and Dharma protectors.

The merit field

In the space at Buddha's right side, on a great gathering of clouds, is seated Maitreya, surrounded by the bodhicitta lineage gurus, presided over by Asanga.

Similarly, in the space at Buddha's left side, on a great gathering of clouds, is seated Manjushri, surrounded by the wisdom lineage gurus, presided over by Nagarjuna.

In the space above and behind Buddha Shakyamuni, seated on a great gathering of clouds, is Vajradhara, surrounded by the close lineage gurus: those gurus who received particular teachings directly from particular deities. Brilliant light is radiating from all the higher beings in the merit field, spreading into all the ten directions, purifying the minds of all beings.

Purifying the Place

Next we purify the place where we invite the merit field. Visualize that your surroundings are transformed into a pure land, without any earthly defects and adorned with various natural beauties, shining like purified lapis lazuli. Now recite the following verse:

> May all lands completely become
> As smooth as the surface of lapis lazuli
> And as even as the palm of my hand
> Without any defects such as thorns and rubble.

Making Offerings

Then contemplate the offerings you have arranged for the buddhas and bodhisattvas as being empty of inherent existence and melting into emptiness. From the space of emptiness they manifest again, in the form of pure offerings filling all the space of the ten directions, like the magnificent offerings created by the miraculous power of the famous bodhisattva Samantabhadra.

Having reflected in this way, recite the following prayer:

> May the entire realm of space be filled
> With the supreme clouds of Samantabhadra's offerings
> And with the offerings of gods and humans,
> Both those that are physically offered
> And those visualized.

Then we bless the offerings we have arranged by reciting the mantra for blessing the offerings three times:

om namo bhagawate, bändze sara parma da na, tathagataya, arahate samyak sambuddhaya, tayata, om bändze bändze, maha bändze, maha tedza bändze, maha biya bändze, maha bodhicitta bändze, maha bodhi mando pa sam da ma na bändze, sarwa karma ah wa ra na bi sho da na bändze soha

We invite all the buddhas, deities, great bodhisattvas, arhats, dakas, dakinis, and Dharma protectors to come from their natural abode. They dissolve into the buddhas and bodhisattvas already visualized in front of us in the merit field.

5. The Seven Limb Prayer and Mandala Offering

We now recite the Seven Limb Prayer and offer the mandala while reciting the Mandala Offering Prayer. These are explained on pages 46, 47, and 50.

While reciting the first limb, which is the practice of prostration, we can get up and prostrate but we usually visualize that our body is multiplied as many times as there are atoms of the earth and we imagine them prostrating to the merit field. Similarly, during the practice of the second limb, we visualize that we have multiplied our body into many gods and goddesses to perform offerings to the buddhas and bodhisattvas in the merit field.

THE SEVEN LIMB PRAYER
I bow down respectfully with my body, speech, and faithful mind,
To all Tathagatas in the ten directions,
Those who have already reached the Tathagata state,
Those who are reaching it at present
And those Tathagatas still to come.
Through the power of Samantabhadra's prayers,
May all buddhas manifest vividly in my mind.
I prostrate to them, multiplying my body
As many times as there are atoms of the earth.
In each atom I visualize as many buddhas as there are atoms,

Surrounded by countless bodhisattvas.
Thus, all space is filled with buddhas and bodhisattvas.
I praise all buddhas through magnificent chanting,
Expressing the great ocean of their excellent qualities.

To all buddhas I make offerings of various pure flowers, flower
    garlands,
Of music, anointing oils, magnificent light, and fragrant incense.
I make offerings to them of fine garments, perfume, and potpourri,
Piled high as Mount Meru and arranged in the most beautiful way.
I visualize the highest and most extensive offerings
And offer them with great faith to all buddhas.
I prostrate to the buddhas and make offerings to them,
Following the deeds of the great bodhisattva, Samantabhadra.

I confess to you, buddhas,
Whatever negative actions I have done
Due to the power of anger, desire, and ignorance.

I rejoice in the merit of all the buddhas in the ten directions,
Of the great bodhisattvas and Pratyeka buddhas,
Those who have attained arhathood,
Those who have entered the path to arhathood,
And all other beings.

I make requests to all Great Protectors or buddhas
To turn the highest wheel of Dharma,
As the light dispelling the darkness of the beings in the ten
    directions
And leading them gradually to the enlightened state.

I make requests to those buddhas
Intending to pass into parinirvana,
To live long, for as many eons as there are atoms of the earth,
In order to benefit all beings.

I dedicate whatever merit I have gained
From prostrating, making offerings,
Confessing my negativities,
Rejoicing in the virtue of others,
Requesting the buddhas to turn the wheel of Dharma,
Requesting them to live long,
So that I may attain enlightenment
For the sake of all beings.

Then perform the offering of the mandala while reciting the following prayer:

THE MANDALA OFFERING PRAYER

Om vajra bhumi ah hung, greatly powerful golden ground.
Om vajra rekhe ah hung, at the outermost limit a circular iron
    mountain chain surrounds Mount Meru, king of mountains.

In the east is the continent Lüpagpo,
In the south the continent Dzambuling,
In the west the continent Balangchö,
In the north the continent Draminyän.
At the two sides of the eastern continent are two subcontinents Lü
    and Lüpag,
At the two sides of the southern continent are two subcontinents
    Ngayab and Ngayabzhän,
At the sides of the western continent are two subcontinents Yoden
    and Lamchogdro,
At the sides of the northern continent are two subcontinents
    Draminyän and Draminyängyida.
Precious mountain, wish-granting tree, wish-fulfilling cow, and
    uncultivated crops.

Precious wheel, precious jewel, precious queen, precious minister,
    precious elephant, precious horse, precious general, and great
    treasure vase.

Goddess of grace, goddess of garlands, goddess of song, goddess of
dance, goddess of flowers, goddess of incense, goddess of light,
and goddess of perfume.

Sun, moon, precious umbrella, and banner of victory in every
direction,
And in the center, all the prosperity and possessions of gods and
humans.

This magnificent and glorious collection, encompassing all pros-
perity and goodness,
I offer to you, my most kind root Guru,
To all other holy lineage gurus,
In particular to you, Buddha Shakyamuni,
Together with the entire assembly of the merit field.
Please accept this offering for the welfare of all sentient beings,
And, having accepted it, with your great kindness,
Please bestow your blessings and inspiration on me
And all mother beings throughout space.

Short Mandala Offering
By virtue of offering to you, assembly of buddhas
Visualized before me, this mandala built on a base,
Resplendent with flowers, sprinkled with perfumed water,
Adorned with Mount Meru and the four continents,
As well as the sun and moon.
May all sentient beings share in its good effects.

Om idam guru ratna mandalakam niryatayami
I send forth this jeweled mandala to you, precious Gurus.

Explanation of the Seven Limb Prayer
There are seven parts to this prayer: (1) prostration to the objects of our
inspiration, visualized in the merit field; (2) making offerings to the
buddhas and bodhisattvas; (3) purification of the negative actions that we
have committed; (4) rejoicing in the merit of other beings; (5) requesting

the buddhas and bodhisattvas living in all the ten directions to turn the wheel of Dharma in order to disperse the darkness of all beings; (6) requesting the buddhas and bodhisattvas to live long so that they can guide us all from suffering to enlightenment; (7) dedication of whatever merit we have achieved to benefit all sentient beings.

The purpose of practicing the path to enlightenment is to gain realizations of higher states of mind, such as the understanding of emptiness and bodhicitta. Gaining such realizations is not only a matter of meditation alone, as many experienced yogis have stressed. It is equally important to purify our negative actions and accumulate merit or positive energy. In this way we prepare our mind so that it can be transformed into the experience of higher realizations. Therefore, it is highly recommended that we carry out these practices prior to any meditation on the path.

Although there are many different systems of purification and accumulating merit in Buddhist traditions, the Seven Limb Prayer has unique significance because it comprises all necessary prerequisites. Hence, most yogis in both the sutra and tantra lineages recommend this prayer for these practices.

The Seven Limb Prayer contains four important factors: accumulating merit; increasing the merit we have already gained; preserving our merit and purifying whatever negative actions we have accumulated.

The first, second, fifth, and sixth limbs—prostration, making offerings, requesting higher beings to turn the wheel of Dharma, and requesting them to live long—deal with the factor of accumulating merit. The fourth limb—rejoicing in the merit of others—deals with the factor of increasing our merit. The seventh limb—dedicating our merit—is related to the factor of preserving our merit. And lastly, the third limb—purification of our negative actions—is related to the last factor of purification. Therefore, we can clearly see how the Seven Limb Prayer reveals the essence of all the methods for purifying and increasing our merit.

Many of us are hardly able to achieve any experience in meditation, even after much exertion. This is simply because we lack these kinds of prerequisites. The Seventh Dalai Lama often advised us "not to jump into meditation straight away, without being sure you have prepared your mind so that it is mature enough to gain realizations." Kadampa lamas always say:

Meditating on profound subjects without purifying our negative actions is like planting seed for a precious crop without clearing up the field. And meditating without having enough merit to mature our mind is like expecting a rich crop without supplying good soil and water.

These instructions are very important—we should never forget them!

It is much more effective to recite the Seven Limb Prayer when we clearly understand the significance of each part. Prostration has great meaning. In Tibetan it is *chag tsel*, translated from the Sanskrit word *namo*. *Chag* denotes the buddhas' and bodhisattvas' great attainment of pure body, speech, and mind. *Tsel* means to devote. *Chag tsel* together means: I devote myself sincerely to following the right path, so that I may achieve the same state as the buddhas and bodhisattvas.

The great Pabongka states, "Prostration has such extensive and profound meaning that we can practice the whole Mahayana path in its context."

There are three different ways of prostrating. The first one is as follows: at our heart we join our hands and fold the thumbs in, to form a lotus. We imagine we are holding a most precious jewel, the jewel of enlightenment. The joined hands symbolize the inseparable practice of compassion and wisdom. By prostrating in this way, we are saying that we devote ourselves to attaining the precious state of enlightenment for the sake of all beings.

The second way of prostrating is the short-length prostration. The third is the full-length prostration. When we practice these we start by placing our joined hands, as above, in sequence at the crown of our head, at our forehead, throat, and heart. These positions have great significance: placing our joined hands at our crown indicates that we aspire to obtain the auspicious mark of Buddha's crown, which symbolizes giving protection to all beings. Holding our joined hands at our forehead means that we aspire to obtain the omniscient state, so that we can see the suffering nature of all beings. Holding our joined hands at our throat means that we aspire to achieve the power of giving perfect teachings to all beings in order to liberate them from samsara. Holding the hands at our heart signifies our wish to obtain the highest state of the Dharmakaya, the highest development of wisdom, for the sake of liberating all beings.

Having placed our hands in sequence at these four places, we then go down on our knees and touch the ground with our forehead or prostrate with the full length of our body. This action signifies our complete dedication to stay in samsara in order to help all mother beings. Then we raise our body and stand upright again. This signifies that we will bring all our mother beings from cyclic existence into the enlightened state.

EXPLANATION OF THE MANDALA OFFERING

All experienced yogis find the mandala offering a very important practice for gaining merit. We need this so that we can easily gain the experience of whatever aspect of the path we meditate on.

Once, Atisha's chief disciple, Dromtön Rinpoche, went to visit one of his own main disciples, Gonba Rinchen. When he arrived, Dromtön found that the mandala objects were covered by dust in the corner of the meditation room. This made him unhappy and he scolded Gonba Rinchen, saying, "Why aren't you practicing mandala offering?" Gonba Rinchen answered respectfully, "Today I forgot to offer the mandala because I was deeply involved in my meditation." Dromtön Rinpoche started laughing and said, "Are you a better meditator than Atisha? Although he has reached very high realizations, he still never forgets the practice of offering the mandala every day!"

The life-story of Lama Tsonghkapa also shows us the importance of this practice. After he had received many teachings on sutra and tantra from various gurus, Tsonghkapa asked the great Manjushri many important questions through one of his gurus, Lama Omapa. He questioned him on profound subjects in the practice of tantra, such as subtle emptiness and the illusory body. Manjushri advised Tsonghkapa to leave scholarly activities and to do solitary practice for the purpose of purification and increasing merit.

As Manjushri advised, the great Tsonghkapa went to a solitary place in South Tibet called Oka. There, for many years, he single-pointedly dedicated his life to purification and the practice of offering the mandala. As a result, without much effort, Tsonghkapa later gained many higher realizations on both the sutra and highest tantra paths.

Pabongka Rinpoche often said:

A mandala offering

As Lord Buddha clearly prophesied, the great Tsonghkapa had already attained enlightenment many eons ago. He had no need to purify negative actions. However, to set us a good example, he showed that even after he had reached the highest realizations, he still practiced the prerequisites of purification and accumulation of merit.

There are three kinds of mandala offering: external, internal, and secret. The last two are related to the practice of tantric meditation. The mandala offering that we practice here, the external one, is based on sutra practice.

This mandala offering is the symbolic offering of the prosperity of the whole universe. Therefore, every possible offering we can make is contained in it. For this reason, it is considered a very effective method of accumulating merit. The visualization of the universe, which is generated in this mandala offering, is based on the description of the universe given in traditional Buddhist cosmology.

According to this traditional Buddhist world system, the center of the universe is Mount Meru, surrounded by seven golden mountain chains. Mount Meru has eight levels of ground, four of which are below the ocean and four above it. On the highest level is the palace of Indra, king of the gods in the desire realm. On the great ocean around Mount Meru are four continents and eight subcontinents. The great ocean rests on a golden ground and is surrounded by an iron fence. The sun and moon rotate in space around Mount Meru above the continents.

How to Offer a Mandala

Traditionally, when we perform this mandala offering, we use a mandala base, three or four rings placed on top of each other, a top, grain, and, if we have any, semi-precious stones to pile up on the mandala base. All these symbolize our offering the universe as described in the Mandala Offering Prayer. The important thing in this practice is to visualize as clearly as possible the whole structure of the universe and the precious offerings as they are described.

The base symbolizes the golden ground of the world system; the first ring is the iron fence and the continents; the top two or three rings represent the levels of Mount Meru above the ocean; the mandala top symbolizes the precious things in the whole universe, as well as our own inner virtues, which we offer. Having built the mandala offering on the base, we hold it at the level of our heart. Our left and right hands symbolize Brahma and Indra, who are considered to be the most powerful symbolic kings of the universe.

To build the mandala (see illustration on page 55), first take some grain in your left hand and hold the mandala base. Take some grain with your right hand and put it on the base. Then wipe it with your right forearm in a clockwise direction, tipping the grain away from you. Repeat this three times, visualizing that you are purifying your incorrect motivation. Then put more grain on the base and wipe it in an anti-clockwise direction three times, tipping the grain toward yourself. At the same time visualize that you are receiving great blessings from the merit field to open your mind so that you can offer the mandala from your heart.

Then spread some grain over the base. This symbolizes covering the golden ground with precious jewels. While doing this, recite the mantra *om vajra bhumi ah hung*, meaning "indestructible ground." This is the mantra for blessing the ground of the universe.

Then place the first ring on the base. Take more grain with the right hand and sprinkle it around the inside of the ring, reciting the mantra *om vajra rekhe ah hung*. The ring and the sprinkling of grain symbolize blessing the iron fence that encircles the universe. Next, pile some grain in the middle of the base (1). This symbolizes Mount Meru and the seven golden mountain chains around it.

Then put some grain in the east of the base (2). There are two systems of where the east is held: either on our side of the base or on the side of the merit field, whichever we choose. If we perform the mandala offering with the aim of receiving blessing power from the merit field, then the east is held on our side. And if we perform it with the purpose of accumulating merit, then the east is held on the side of the merit field. Having put grain in the east, we then put some in the south (3), west (4), and north (5). These four points symbolize the four major continents around Mount Meru. Now put some grain at each side of the eastern continent (6, 7), then likewise to each side of the other continents to symbolize the eight subcontinents or islands (8–13).

The next step is to build the visualization of the four unique precious things that are contained on the four continents. They are: in the east the precious mountain (14), in the south the precious tree (15), in the west the precious cow (16), and in the north the naturally growing precious crops (17). To symbolize these four we put grain in each of these places.

After this we build the visualization of the eight precious objects belonging to a wheel-turning king who rules the four continents. Place the second ring on the top of the first ring that is already filled with grain. Beginning in the east (18), put some grain in the eight directions inside the second ring (18–25). These symbolize the eight precious things: the seven auspicious royal objects plus the great treasure vase, as described in the prayer. They are visualized in the space above the continents and islands around Mount Meru.

If we are using three rings we continue on the second ring here, but if we are using four rings we put the third ring on here and then put grain in the eight directions again (26–33). These symbolize the eight goddesses carrying eight different types of offerings. These offerings are visualized on the four levels of Mount Meru above the sea.

Now place the last ring on the grain and inside it put some grain toward your left and right hand (34, 35), symbolizing the sun and moon. Then put some grain away from you and toward you (36, 37), symbolizing the protection umbrella and victory banner. The victory banner symbolizes victory over inner evil. As we generally make mandala offerings mainly for the purpose of receiving blessing power from the buddhas and bodhisattvas, we normally place the banner of victory toward us. If, however, we feel there is some obstacle to our meditation practice, it is suggested that we put the protection umbrella toward us—this symbolizes receiving protection from the buddhas and bodhisattvas.

Finally place the mandala top in the middle (38). This symbolizes the offerings of Samantabhadra. We visualize on the top of Mount Meru an enormous precious tree with many branches spreading throughout space. On each branch is the bodhisattva Samantabhadra, creating from his concentration power innumerable priceless offerings to the buddhas and bodhisattvas that we visualize in the merit field.

We then transform the entire universe that we have visualized into a pure universe. Holding the mandala at our heart, we offer it to the merit field.

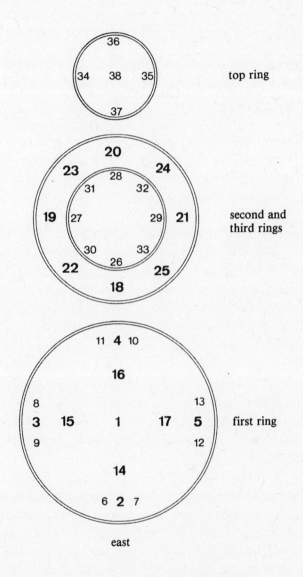

Placing the heaps of grain for the mandala offering

6. Requesting the Merit Field to Bestow the Power of Their Blessings

Still holding the mandala at our heart, we make requests to the buddhas and bodhisattvas to bless our mind to be able to achieve the realization of the path we are meditating on, as follows:

O buddhas and bodhisattvas, please bestow your boundless compassion, stainless wisdom, and limitless power upon me, so that I may quickly gain realization of the path I am meditating on, in order to attain enlightenment for the sake of all my mother sentient beings.

Having made our request, we tip the grain toward us thinking that we are receiving their blessings. Visualize that from their hearts emanate brilliant white light and nectar, which enter through our crown chakra, completely filling our body and mind and purifying all obstacles formed by our negative karma and delusions that hinder us from gaining realizations.

Then all other buddhas, bodhisattvas, deities, arhats, dakas, dakinis, and Dharma protectors gradually dissolve into Buddha Shakyamuni, who is inseparable from your own guru. Finally, Buddha Shakyamuni comes above your head. In his heart visualize a moon disc surrounded by the syllables of his mantra: *om muni muni mahamuniye svaha.* Recite this one hundred times. Outside this mantra is the mantra of Tsonghkapa, which represents the mantra of your own guru: *om ah guru vajradhara sumati kiti siddhi hung hung.* Recite this one hundred times, too.

At this point we do the actual meditation on whatever aspect of the path we are contemplating. When the meditation is over, we dissolve the merit field as follows: visualize your heart in the form of an open lotus; then Guru Shakyamuni descends through your crown chakra into your body and sits inside the lotus. Think that he becomes inseparable from your mind.

To sum up: this tradition of practicing the gradual path to enlightenment has two stages: the preparation stage, which consists of the six preliminary practices, and the actual meditation. This system should be applied to all practices of meditation on the path, from meditation on the precious human rebirth to meditation on emptiness.

PART TWO

Meditations on the Initial Level
of Inner Development

Maitreya

6. The Precious Human Rebirth

At this time we have gained the precious human rebirth. How fortunate we are! How rare it is to gain! With it we can achieve something much more meaningful than the temporary happiness of this life.

We have obtained such a precious rebirth this time—there is no guarantee that we will find it again. We have great potential not only to achieve the continuation of this happy rebirth into many future lifetimes, but also to attain enlightenment. Then we will be able to lead countless beings from the suffering of cyclic existence, as well as freeing ourselves.

However, if we allow ourselves to be tempted by the pleasures of life and neglect such a precious opportunity and waste it, there is no greater loss to us than this. No matter how much material pleasure we may gain in this life, it is only useful for us as long as we live. Sooner or later death will definitely come and, when it does, nothing will be of any value except our pure inner virtues.

In his *Letter to a Disciple* Nagarjuna says:

> Just as many elephants suffer great loss of life in attempting to get fresh new shoots from high mountain cliffs because of their desire, likewise beings fall into the sufferings of the lower realms again and again as a result of their non-virtuous karma, accumulated under the influence of great desire for the little pleasures they may gain when they are born in the higher realms.

Kadampa Geshe Chen Ngawa, who was the first to carry on the teachings of the stages of the path from Dromtön Rinpoche, always reminded everyone of the following verse by Chandrakirti:

> If we do not try to free ourselves from suffering
> When we are free from the lower realms this time alone
> And have all the favorable conditions to be able to practice
>   Dharma,
> What can help us later, when we fall into the bottomless abyss
> Of the lower realms where we have no power?

Therefore, we should remind ourselves of how fortunate we are, and how important it is for us to achieve something more meaningful now that we have this rare opportunity. If we are truthful and sincere with ourselves, we will do so.

Many great yogis in the past, such as Milarepa and Tsonghkapa, gained enlightenment within one lifetime. They started off with nothing more than we have now—a precious human rebirth—so we too can achieve the same results. Master Pawo, who was the chief disciple of Aryadeva, Nagarjuna's first successor, says:

> If we obtain the perfect human rebirth, we gain the incredible ability, not only to free ourselves from the suffering of cyclic existence forever, but also to gain the state of enlightenment, liberating countless beings from suffering. There is nothing to compare with this precious human rebirth. Who would waste such a rebirth?

It is extremely difficult to gain such a rebirth again. We did not gain this perfect vehicle by chance; we had to accomplish many rare causes and conditions to have this precious fruit. Buddha says:

> To obtain the precious human rebirth, the very least we have to do is to practice morality and the six perfections purely for a whole lifetime. And this is very difficult.

Kadampa lamas say:

If we carefully look within, we will see that our minds are dominated by delusions most of the time, so it is difficult to keep morality purely for a whole lifetime. Therefore we can hardly expect to be reborn as a human being. We should not waste our valuable time. How difficult it is to gain such a rare rebirth! Yet we have gained it this time. It is a miracle that we have, for the causes are so rare.

While Buddha was teaching once, he touched the dusty ground with the tip of his finger and, holding it up, said:

The number of beings who are reborn in the higher realms, from the higher as well as the lower realms, resembles the specks of dust on my fingertip. The number of beings who take rebirth in the lower realms resembles the specks of dust on the great earth.

So many more beings are born in the lower realms. It is crucial that we make use of this rare opportunity in a meaningful way. Another analogy of Buddha's shows how fortunate we are:

Imagine a great ocean, at the bottom of which lives a blind turtle. A golden yoke floats on the surface of the ocean, moved at random by the winds and the currents. The turtle comes to the surface only once in every hundred years. Can you imagine how rare it would be for the turtle to surface anywhere near the golden yoke, let alone actually encircle his head in it? Finding the precious human rebirth is even more rare than this.

Here the ocean symbolizes cyclic existence. The blind turtle stands for the beings within samsara, their minds blinded by delusion: they are unable to see what the cause of suffering is, or the way they can liberate themselves from suffering. The fact that the blind turtle mostly stays at the bottom of the ocean, coming to its surface only once in every hundred years, shows that beings mostly take rebirth in the lower realms, rarely having the chance to appear in the higher realms. The golden yoke symbolizes the appearance of the Buddha's teachings. The yoke's random movement by the winds and tides indicates that they do not stay in one place, but move from one place to another.

What makes our human rebirth so precious is having what are known as eight freedoms and ten endowments. They give us the tremendous opportunity to practice Buddhadharma.

The Eight Freedoms

1   Freedom from being born in the animal realm.
2   Freedom from being born in the realm of hungry ghosts or impoverished beings.
3   Freedom from being born in a hell realm.
4   Freedom from being born as a long-life god, where there is more temptation to prevent us from practicing Dharma.
5   Freedom from being born in a place where it is impossible to meet the Dharma.
6   Freedom from being born at a time when there is no Dharma.
7   Freedom from being born in a barbaric place, where we cannot practice Dharma freely.
8   Freedom from being born with defective organs, which would make it difficult to practice Dharma.

The Ten Endowments

1   Being born as a human being.
2   Being born in a place where we can meet the Dharma.
3   Being born with a perfectly functioning body.
4   Not having committed the five heinous crimes.
5   Having faith in the Dharma.
6   Being born in the fortunate period when Buddha has appeared.
7   Being born in the fortunate period when Buddha has taught the Dharma.
8   Being born in the fortunate period when the Dharma still exists.
9   Being born in the fortunate period when material facilities to practice Dharma are available.

10 Being born in the fortunate period when we are still able to
   meet pure followers of the Buddha's teachings.

The great Tsonghkapa emphasized that we should remind ourselves of
these eighteen achievements again and again, so that we will always be
enthusiastic about practicing pure Buddhadharma. In this way we will be
able to fulfill the great essence of finding this precious human rebirth.

Shantideva also pointed out:

> Suppose a merchant sails across a great ocean to a distant island,
> where precious jewels can be found. He travels for many years, risk-
> ing his life to get there. He finally arrives there, finds the jewels,
> but returns empty-handed. How mindless that would be! And yet,
> it would be much more regrettable if we were to fall back into the
> suffering of the lower realms without having achieved anything dur-
> ing this precious human life.

Meditation on the Precious Human Rebirth

After performing the preliminary practices, we should contemplate in
this way:

How fortunate I am, through finding this precious human rebirth, to have
such incredible opportunities. It is even possible for me to achieve enlightenment within this lifetime.

Imagine how I would be if I had been born in the animal realm, as a
hungry ghost, or in a hell realm. Animals' minds are completely dull, they
have no wisdom as we have, and cannot understand any deeper meanings,
so how could they practice Dharma? Hungry ghosts suffer from terrible
hunger and thirst, so how could they even begin to think about Dharma?
The sufferings that hell beings experience are unimaginable and immeasurable. So I am very lucky at the moment, because I am free from such miserable conditions.

Although beings in the god realms have no such sufferings, they do have
incredible temptations, and it is very hard for them to turn their minds to

Dharma. Now I am also free from being born in a place where I can easily fall under the influence of such powerful temptations. I have been born in the human realm, the perfect place to practice Dharma purely.

However, I could have been born as a human during the dark period, for instance, before Dharma appeared in the world. Or I could be born as a human later, when Buddhadharma has disappeared; then I would not be able to meet it. Similarly, if I had been born in a barbaric place, I would be unable to practice Dharma freely; or not at all if I had been born where there is no Dharma. Or if I had been born with seriously defective organs, it would also be difficult for me to practice Dharma properly.

How fortunate I am! At the moment I am free from those unhappy situations. I have been born as a human being, in a place where I can meet the Dharma and with the physical and mental ability to practice it. I have no strong obstacles caused by my having committed the five heinous crimes. I have faith in Buddhadharma. Buddha has come and given teachings and they still exist. Therefore I have been able to meet the pure Buddhadharma. There are still many pure Dharma practitioners, followers of Lord Buddha's teachings, so that I can always be inspired in my practice. Even the material facilities that allow me to practice Dharma are available.

If I am truthful and sincere with myself, I should not waste such a precious opportunity. I must practice Dharma purely. Through finding this precious human rebirth, I have incredible potential and can achieve the continuation of the human rebirth into many lifetimes. What is more, I also have the chance to become completely free from the suffering of cyclic existence forever. I can even achieve enlightenment within this lifetime. Therefore this human rebirth that I have found is most precious to me. It not only gives me such incredible opportunities, but is also extremely difficult to find again—in fact, it is almost impossible. How mindless I would be if I were to waste such a precious rebirth!

O Guru Buddha Shakyamuni, please bestow the blessings of your wisdom, compassion, and power on me, so that I may realize the value of this precious human rebirth.

Having contemplated in this way, visualize white light coming from the white syllable *om* inside Buddha Shakyamuni's crown chakra. The light dissolves into your own crown chakra and, filling your whole body, purifies all the imprints accumulated through the negative actions of your body.

Then visualize red light coming from the red syllable *ah* shining radiantly at Buddha's throat chakra. The light dissolves into your own throat chakra, purifying all the imprints accumulated through your negative actions of speech.

Blue light comes from the blue syllable *hum* inside Buddha Shakyamuni's heart chakra and dissolves into your own heart chakra, purifying all the negative imprints accumulated through your deluded states of mind.

Finally from the heart of Guru Buddha Shakyamuni, who is inseparably one with your own guru, white light together with pure nectar comes and enters your own crown chakra, completely filling your body. Firmly think at this stage that you have received immense blessing power from Guru Buddha Shakyamuni.

7. Awareness of Impermanence

It is only when we realize the truth of impermanence that we can seriously turn our minds toward Dharma and practice it continuously and purely. As a result we will eventually accomplish great benefit. Lord Buddha says:

> There is no greater realization than being aware of the impermanence of this life. Just as the elephant's footprint is the biggest of all animal's footprints, so is meditation on impermanence the most powerful meditation.

If we are not aware of the impermanent nature of our life, then we can easily be deceived by the temptations of desire and attachment to happiness within this life—a happiness that is short-lived and superficial. We would waste our incredible human potential and would face unbearable regret at the time of death. Then it would be too late to do anything about it. Therefore it is extremely important to remind ourselves of death again and again, so that we are inspired to achieve something much more meaningful for our future, through the incredible potentials that we have as human beings. Karmapa Rinpoche, one of Tsonghkapa's teachers when he was young, says:

> We do not bother about death while we are alive. When death comes, we start to scream, tearing at our chests with unbearable fear. Be afraid now of death—now, when there is something we can do about it. Then, when death comes, we will be able to pass away in peace and with great joy.

There is hardly any other awareness that has such power, compelling us to make good use of our lives by practicing Dharma purely. The temptations of less meaningful or trivial worldly activities lose their hold and we stop wasting our precious energy. Kadampa lamas always say:

> Meditation on tantric deities such as Guhyasamaja, Heruka, or Yamantaka is not profound, but meditation on impermanence is. If we single-pointedly meditate on impermanence, we will be able to achieve all realizations without much effort.

One day, Dromtön Rinpoche taught in Redreng, to the north of Lhasa, the capital of Tibet. While he was walking in the woods, he saw a man circumambulating a stupa, the symbol of Buddha's inner qualities. The man asked Rinpoche whether he was doing it correctly. Rinpoche smiled and said, "I rejoice in your actions, but I wish you would practice pure Dharma." Then the man thought, "I had better do prostrations." The next time Dromtön Rinpoche met him, the man asked whether he was prostrating correctly. Rinpoche answered, "What you are doing is very good, but it would be even better if you tried to practice pure Dharma." Again the man thought he was not doing the correct practice, so he started to recite mantras. The next day Dromtön Rinpoche passed by again and found the man reciting a mantra of higher tantra. He said to Rinpoche, "Now I am practicing pure Dharma." Dromtön Rinpoche folded his hands together and said, "I really appreciate your recitation of highest mantra, but pure Dharma has to do with motivation. If your mind is still dominated by desire for selfish material gain and fame, then whatever you practice can hardly be the pure practice of Dharma. Please try to overcome this first, by being aware of impermanence and death."

The man took Rinpoche's advice to heart and meditated with single-pointed concentration on death and impermanence. Soon, without much effort, he was able to achieve many high realizations.

Although we may practice meditation on emptiness, bodhicitta, or even the highest tantras, we can still be easily tempted by desire for fame or some material gain, unless we are constantly aware of death and impermanence. Without this awareness, we cannot overcome the unhappiness and dissatisfaction that desire and attachment cause. Also our practice would not be pure Dharma. If our motivation is impure, dominated by selfish desire, then no matter how much higher Dharma we practice, or for how long, it will not help us when we die. If we are truly concerned about the critical situation at the time of death, then it is of course extremely important never to forget that we may die at any moment and remember how we are approaching death moment by moment. Lama Tsonghkapa says:

> Meditation on death is not only important for us at the initial stage, when we first begin to practice Dharma; it is equally important to continue meditation on death even on reaching the higher stages of realization.

And similarly, Kadampa Lama Gyama Rinpoche said:

> If I forget to meditate on death early in the morning, my whole morning practice becomes impure. If I forget to meditate on death at midday, my whole afternoon's meditation practice becomes impure.

All these instructions given by experienced Buddhist yogis are extremely beneficial. We should try to follow them. As Shantideva says:

> From the time of our birth we are already inside the cemetery. If we contemplate our bodies, we can realize that our corpse is already with us.

Having performed the preliminary practices (see pages 35–56), we should reflect in this way:

Meditation on the Awareness of Death

How important it is for me to practice pure Dharma. It is inevitable that, sooner or later, death will come to me. There is no way to escape death, no matter whether we are learned or not, rich or poor, or whether we have power or not; we are all equally powerless at the time of death. Leaving everything behind, we must all travel alone. At the time of death, nothing can help me; my only hope lies in my being able to practice Dharma purely while I am alive.

Not only is death inevitable, but there is no certainty about when it will occur. At any time from today, there could be an unfortunate situation in which I could lose my life. This happens every day to many people. The lifespan of human beings on this planet is not fixed, so I do not know how much longer my life will last. Furthermore, every day we inevitably come across dangers that can cause death at any time and at any place. The human body is so fragile that even slightly unconducive conditions can destroy it. I am extremely lucky to have survived until now, despite such dangerous circumstances. If I am not mindless, I shall practice the Dharma purely from now on, without wasting precious time.

O my Guru Buddha Shakyamuni, please bestow the blessings of your wisdom, compassion, and power on me, so that I may become continually aware of impermanence and death. Thus, I shall be able to carry on pure Dharma practice throughout my life.

Having contemplated in this way, visualize white light coming from the heart of Guru Buddha Shakyamuni and entering into your heart chakra. As soon as the light penetrates your body, all your negative actions and their imprints, which are in the form of darkness, vanish just as the darkness of the earth disappears when the sun rises.

Once again, from the heart of Guru Buddha Shakyamuni, white light and nectar enter and descend through your crown chakra, completely filling your body with pure nectar. Feel great joy and think that you have received tremendous blessings from Guru Buddha Shakyamuni, who is inseparable from your guru.

Buddha Shakyamuni teaching

8. Taking Refuge in the Three Jewels

Taking refuge in the Three Jewels means fully opening our mind to the Jewel of Buddha by understanding that buddhas, or Enlightened Ones, are our perfect guides; to the Jewel of Dharma, the teachings shown by Buddha, by understanding that it is the perfect path leading us as well as others beyond suffering; to the Jewel of Sangha, or spiritual friends, by understanding that they are fully qualified in helping us to improve our inner understanding through their great inspiration.

At the moment we are in a higher realm where we can enjoy many pleasures, yet if we carefully examine our seemingly happy situation we will see that it is totally subject to impermanence. Regardless of our desire not to be separated from the material pleasures that we can enjoy here, there is no way for us to retain our present human state for long. At the time of our departure from this life into the next, we inevitably have to leave our present conditions behind and fall completely at the mercy of our own karma and delusion. To quote Lama Tsonghkapa:

When we are in a temporary state of happiness, most of us hardly ever think of our impermanent life situation: that soon we have to depart, leaving everything behind when we pass on to the next life. And so we unfortunately become trapped into clinging to this temporary happiness and do not bother to practice pure Dharma, which is the only thing of value to us when we die—a most critical time for us. Hence, if we are wise enough, from now on we will try to realize the suffering nature of our lives. This is extremely important.

Let us imagine how much sorrow we would experience on leaving everything behind at the time of death. You see, our future happiness depends on the kind of rebirth we take. When the time comes for us to depart from this life to the next, we cannot choose where we will go. We are totally at the mercy of the karma we have accumulated. Wherever it impels us, we have no choice but to go. We are completely powerless. How critical this time will be for us!

Lord Buddha says:

> Non-virtuous actions will lead us to take rebirth in the lower realms of the animals, the hungry ghosts, or hell. Virtuous actions will lead us to take rebirth in the higher realms of humans, gods, or demi-gods.

If we are totally honest with ourselves and closely check up on the mental attitudes we have had since our childhood, we will see that our minds have mostly been uncontrollably dominated by negative thoughts of anger, attachment, jealousy, pride, and so on. Under such conditions we are naturally more inclined to carry out non-virtuous actions through our speech, body, and mind. In this way we have accumulated many more non-virtuous karma than virtuous ones. Furthermore, the amount of non-virtuous karma we have accumulated since beginningless time is unimaginable.

Unless we manage to purify all this negative action through practicing pure Dharma, there is hardly any hope for us not to fall into the immeasurable suffering of rebirth in the lower realms. Even if we are able to gain rebirth in a higher realm, we still have the same situation. Whatever prosperity we have is subject to decay and again we will have to face the same critical situation. Shantideva says:

> If we remain careless when we have this tremendous opportunity to develop virtuous states for the sake of our future happiness, then when this present happy state is over and we face the critical time of death, there is nothing we can do but fall at the mercy of our karma.

Therefore it is crucial for us to be aware of the fact that we have an immeasurable amount of non-virtuous karma, yet very little of the virtuous karma that could help us. Having realized this, we should sincerely seek the right path to release ourselves from such suffering. Similarly, the great Indian master, Dignaga, says:

> From beginningless time we have all been powerlessly drowning in the ageless and bottomless ocean of cyclic existence; we suffer endlessly from being tortured by the various ruthless monsters of our delusions. Hence, how vital it is for us to search for whoever can release us from this unimaginable suffering without any delay.

What is more, awareness of the suffering nature of life not only inspires us to purify our negative karma and accumulate virtuous karma, thus enabling us to achieve the continuation of the human rebirth and eventually total freedom from cyclic existence, it is also the only method to control the craziness of our minds now; we are always restless, rushing around everywhere without any satisfaction. Kadampa Geshe Chen Ngawa always reminds us:

> Unless we look more deeply into our impermanent nature and uncertain situation and thus see the nature of suffering, we can hardly appreciate whatever fortunate state we have at the moment and be content. Without contentment, we can never enjoy our lives, however many material comforts we may have.

Shantideva also mentions the advantages of being aware of suffering:

> Unless we control the craziness of our unceasing desire, there is no way for us to gain tranquility and peace. The only way to control desire is by being aware of the suffering nature of life. Furthermore, realization of suffering kelps us to endure whatever hardship and difficulties we have to face. It also reduces our pride and helps us to develop great sympathy toward those who experience similar sufferings.

Lama Tsonghkapa says:

> Looking into the nature of suffering is, in fact, seeking the right
> way to attain peace and true happiness.

Therefore it is very important for us to meditate on the suffering nature of
cyclic existence. To quote Nagarjuna:

> We should remind ourselves every day of the suffering of animals;
> of the hungry ghosts suffering from unbearable thirst and hunger;
> of the hell beings suffering from unbearable extremes of cold and
> heat. And then we should be heedful to maintain virtuous actions
> of body, speech, and mind, day and night.

Why We Should Take Refuge in the Three Jewels

Who has the true ability to guide us toward total freedom from the suffering of cyclic existence? Upon investigation, we will clearly realize that
only Enlightened Ones do. They themselves have reached beyond the suffering of cyclic existence and their minds are full of boundless, unceasing
compassion toward those still caught in it. To quote the great Indian master, Pawo:

> Unless we are mindless, we should take as our guides those who
> have fully cast away all faults and accomplished all perfect qualities
> and follow their instructions.

Tsonghkapa beautifully illustrates four reasons to show how and why
Enlightened Ones should be taken as our perfect guides:

Firstly, just as those who are themselves sunk in a mire can have no
power to pull out others, despite their sympathy, so we can hardly help
those who are suffering in cyclic existence, unless we ourselves become
totally free from suffering. Enlightened Ones have completely reached
beyond the suffering of cyclic existence through realizing the truth of suffering, the truth of the cause of suffering, the truth of the cessation of suffering, and the truth of the path to the cessation of suffering.

Secondly, having generated great compassion to liberate all beings from suffering, they have accomplished measureless merit by spending three countless eons practicing extensive wisdom and skillful means. Thus their minds are boundlessly empowered by great compassion and love toward all. Master Pawo says:

All beings' minds are overpowered by delusions. However, your mind, my great Guru Buddha Shakyamuni, is completely boundless with great compassion in order to liberate us from the chains of delusion. Your compassion toward all beings cannot even be compared to the compassion of a mother for her only child.

Thirdly, since Enlightened Ones have completely eliminated any kind of partiality, their minds are equally well-disposed toward all, whether beings try to harm them or love them.

Fourthly, Enlightened Ones are perfectly expert in understanding the mental disposition of each and every sentient being and the teachings most suitable for them. Thus they are perfect guides who can lead us to liberation from suffering. We should take refuge in the buddhas.

As Buddha says:

Sufferings originate from nowhere else but our own unsubdued mind. If we wish to achieve a true state of happiness, the best way is to train ourselves in eliminating our negative states of mind.

We cannot gain a true and stable state of happiness unless we subdue the craziness of our own mind. If we remain careless and ignore the bad influence of delusions on our mind, this will lead us to accumulate endless negative actions. No matter how happy a rebirth we have gained now, nothing is stable, all is subject to decay. As a result of negative karma, we again fall back endlessly into the suffering of the lower realms. Therefore, if we are wise enough, we will see that there is nothing more important than to seek the true way that can lead to the stable and lasting happiness beyond the temptations of cyclic existence.

Shantideva says:

The immense fires and burning iron ground of the hell realms are not somebody's creation, but arise from the evil thoughts within our minds. All the horrors that exist on the earth arise from the evil minds of beings. Thus, if we can conquer the craziness of our mind, we will have conquered the whole of cyclic existence.

If we wish to be free from suffering we must first realize deeply what suffering is and what the root cause is; having understood this, we should then practice the profound means to eliminate the cause. This can only be done when we develop our wisdom, therefore training our mind in wisdom is what truly protects us from suffering. This is what is known as the Jewel of Dharma. We should take refuge in the Jewel of Dharma.

Although Dharma is the true protection from suffering, without constant inspiration from more advanced spiritual friends it is difficult for us to accomplish our Dharma practice. Therefore, we should seek support and great inspiration from the Sangha by following their example of pure practice. We should take refuge in the Jewel of Sangha.

Meditation on Taking Refuge

I have fortunately found the precious human rebirth, which gives me the incredible opportunity to become enlightened within a short time. Yet even this precious rebirth is subject to impermanence. Sooner or later, death will inevitably come to me. Then nothing can protect me from endless suffering, except pure, virtuous karma. Let me be truly honest with myself and check on my present situation.

My mind is always completely dominated by delusions such as anger, attachment, desire, jealousy, pride, and so on. The number of negative thoughts occurring in my mind in one day cannot be counted, not to mention how much negative karma I have accumulated since my childhood. What is more, the amount of negative karma I have accumulated throughout my past lives, since beginningless time, is unthinkable. How can I remain careless and not be concerned with this completely insecure and uncertain situation?

Although I have this happy human state at the moment, I cannot rely on it because I will definitely have to depart from this life soon, leaving everything behind. Even if I accumulate enough virtue to be able to take a higher rebirth, the situation will be the same. Wherever I go and whichever body I take within cyclic existence, all is subject to impermanence. Therefore, if I do not want to allow myself to be fooled by my narrow-minded desire for only temporary pleasures, I shall seek the true guide who can show me the pure path to liberation from cyclic existence before it is too late.

Who is really able to show me the right way to liberate myself from the suffering of cyclic existence? The Enlightened Ones have this ability. Not only have they totally reached beyond the fear of cyclic existence themselves, but their minds are boundless with great compassion toward all beings equally. Furthermore they are perfectly skilled at showing every single being the faultless method that leads them beyond the suffering of cyclic existence. I take refuge in the buddhas.

But Lord Buddha says that having faith in the Buddha is in itself not sufficient to liberate ourselves. The true protector is the practice of Dharma. I shall sincerely try to follow and put into practice whatever teachings Lord Buddha has shown me. In this way I take refuge in the Dharma.

To be able to practice the Dharma sincerely and continuously, I will need constant inspiration from those who are advanced in spiritual practice, therefore I will take refuge in the Sangha, my true spiritual friends.

After reflecting on the need to take refuge we recite the *Reminding Oneself of the Three Jewels Sutra*:

> I venerate Buddha, the Omniscient One, he or she who, having completely abandoned all faults and fully accomplished all virtuous qualities, is Tathagata; who has reached beyond the ocean of cyclic existence, the perfect destroyer of all inner evil, at whose feet even the highest gods and all humans bow down; who has reached the highest happiness, who knows the world perfectly, who is the great conqueror over the evil minds of all beings, who gives perfect guidance to all beings, the highest teacher of all humans and gods.
>
> Tathagatas are the ultimate result of accomplishing the virtuous path; they never waste any virtues; they are beautifully adorned with the strength of great patience; they are great treasurers of merit; they

are uniquely purified with auspicious marks. They give immeasurable joy to whoever sees them, they give endless bliss to the minds of those who are interested in virtue; they conquer all evils by wisdom; their power can never be suppressed by any evil.

I venerate Buddha, the greatest teacher of all beings, father of bodhisattvas, king of all Aryas, perfect guide for those who wish to travel to the city of enlightenment; whose confidence is beyond the comprehension of ordinary beings, whose speech is pure, whose voice perfectly delights, whose body is so beautiful that it brings endless joy to the minds of all beings; who is beyond comparison, whose mind is never defiled by any faults of the desire realm, whose mind is never stained by any faults of the form realm, whose mind is not obscured by any faults of the formless realm. Free from all suffering, liberated from the bondage of the five aggregates, having no fault of any contaminated element, who is perfectly trained in his or her physical and mental conduct, who has completely cut off any evil influence from maras, or evils; who, free from all sorrows, liberated from cyclic existence, having crossed the river of delusions and having fully accomplished wisdom, abides in the wisdom of the past, present, and future buddhas; who does not abide in the state of mere liberation from cyclic existence, but, while remaining in the perfection of the Dharmakaya state, always travels to see the suffering nature of all beings. These are the great qualities of the buddhas.

The Dharma shown by the Tathagata is perfectly wholesome at the initial stage of training our mind when we set out to reach liberation; it is perfectly wholesome at the intermediate stage during the journey; it is perfectly wholesome at the final stage of achieving our destination. The Dharma contains noble meaning and takes the form of noble words; it is not mixed with any faults, it is pure, it is the perfect training, it is beautifully taught by Enlightened Ones. It is that which clearly sees the truth; it is void of any disease of cyclic existence; it is everlasting; it shows the perfect way to liberation; it gives great meaning to those who observe it; it is perfectly qualified through examination by many great scholars; it shows the perfect method described by Buddha; it carries beings toward enlightenment; it is perfectly suitable to the minds of those who seek liberation; it is well-grounded; it enables beings to cut themselves off from all kinds of sufferings.

The Sangha of the Mahayana have entered the true path, they abide in great wisdom, have equalized their minds toward all beings, traveling along the same path through which all buddhas have reached the tathagata state. The Sangha are objects of veneration, objects of homage, the perfect merit field, source of benefit, and the everlasting source of goodness.

Having recited this sutra we should make the following request:

O my Guru Buddha Shakyamuni please bestow the blessings of your wisdom, compassion, and power on me so that I may gain realization of the Three Jewels and thus be able to benefit all mother beings.

Then we visualize that all the buddhas, deities, bodhisattvas, arhats, dakas, dakinis, and Dharma protectors in the merit field show their limitless, unending great compassion and love toward us all.

In front of each of them is the Jewel of Dharma in the form of manuscripts, representing their inexpressible qualities of pure mind, pure body, and pure speech. Brilliant white light radiates from the hearts of all these awakened beings and from the manuscripts.

Light and nectar descend from them and enter your crown chakra, filling your body with light and nectar. All negativities of body, speech, and mind are expelled through your crown chakra in the same way that rising soapy water cleans a dirty glass.

At this stage we should firmly believe that our body, speech, and mind are filled with ceaseless blessings and tremendous bliss.

PART THREE

Meditation on the Medium Level
of Inner Development

Avalokiteshvara

9. The Suffering Nature
of Cyclic Existence

Through maintaining pure morality, as the Enlightened Ones have shown, we can be born again in one of the happy states of the higher realms: the god realm, the human realm, or the realm of the demi-gods. Through such a rebirth we may gain many temporary pleasures, but as Buddha taught:

Birth will end in death.
Youth will end in old age.
Meetings will end in separation.
Wealth will end in loss.
All things in cyclic existence
are transient, impermanent.

Whatever prosperity or pleasure we may achieve within cyclic existence, it is totally subject to decay. It goes without saying that we have been born in the human and god realms countless times. Even the number of times we have been born as Indra, king of the god realm, or as Brahma, king of the three realms, is measureless. But we fall back again and again into the miserable state of rebirth as an animal, a hungry ghost, or a hell being. To quote Shantideva:

From beginningless time we have had the chance to experience many pleasures through being born in the higher realms. Yet, whenever we take rebirth in these realms, we fall back again into the bottomless abyss of the lower realms and experience endless, unbearable sorrows and suffering.

Similarly Nagarjuna says:

> When we have the chance to appear in the human or god realms, having spent countless eons in the darkness of the lower realms, we again start clinging to the temporary pleasure we have gained through that rebirth. We do not realize that this state is subject to decay and thus accumulate ceaseless non-virtues. As a result of this we again fall helplessly into the immeasurable misery of the suffering of the lower realms. In this way we are powerlessly swept by the unchallengeable force of karma and delusions into the endless cycle of rebirths.

Therefore for those who wish to achieve a true state of everlasting happiness there is nothing more important than to realize the uncertainty and impermanence of even the highest rebirth in samsara; and having realized this, to search for the right path that can lead them to true happiness beyond the confused state of cyclic existence. The great master Aryadeva states:

> Wise ones clearly see that even the happiest rebirth in cyclic existence is in the nature of suffering, just like the state of rebirth in the lowest realm. And without realizing the suffering nature of the whole of cyclic existence, there is no way we can turn our mind away from insatiable desire and uncontrollable attachment to the temporary states of happiness that we could gain. We can never reach everlasting peace unless we are able to overcome the craziness of our delusions.

Even in the human or god realms there is no true happiness, not to mention how much we would suffer if we were born in the lower realms. The human realm is full of suffering, as we can observe from our own experience. Our lives begin with the suffering of birth and end with the suffering of death. Although we have this fortunate rebirth at the moment, however much temporary happiness we may have, it is still under the domination of uncontrollable delusions and we are still at the mercy of the force of our karma.

The Eight Types of Suffering in Cyclic Existence

Buddha described humans as being inescapably subject to eight different types of suffering: the sufferings of (1) birth, (2) illness, (3) old age, (4) death, (5) constantly facing undesirable things, (6) being separated from desirable things, (7) not fulfilling our desire, and (8) the suffering of being bound by the chains of the suffering nature of the five aggregates.

1. The Suffering of Birth

The process of conception and birth is full of pain. From the moment of conception until we are born we are trapped inside a very narrow space and suffer as if buried deep in mud, despite our mother's great concern and care. Whenever she drinks or eats something hot we suffer as if being scalded. Likewise, whenever she moves we are squeezed between the bones of her pelvis and feel as if we are being tortured. Whenever she gets up or sits down we are terrified and feel as if we are being hurtled from the ground onto a high hill and back down again into a deep valley. During the nine months we stay in the womb the sufferings we experience are like those of hell.

After nine months we experience unbearable suffering when we are born. Falling into the new world, we are frightened by everything around us. Not only do we suffer from the pains of being born, but birth itself is the source of all basic human suffering. Sickness, old age, and death, all the sufferings we will have to face, originate from birth. Lama Tsonghkapa says:

Since beginningless time we have been undergoing this miserable suffering of birth. Unless we completely eliminate our delusions, which lead to rebirth in cyclic existence, we will ceaselessly have to face the unbearable pain of birth.

2. The Suffering of Illness

Human beings are often tormented by painful mental and physical ill-
nesses. When we are ill and in pain we suddenly lose heart and begin to feel
grief over the collapse of our health. However strong we may be physically, we will become so weak that we cannot even move our limbs properly and fall completely at the mercy of others' support. Our beautiful
bodies turn into ugly skeletons; gradually our bodies become rotten, full
of filth and revolting smells. Even our relatives and friends are afraid to be
near us. Over and above this we constantly have to face unbearable pain
and the fear of death.

From the time we are born until we die, we are always liable to fall into
the misery of illness. But the disease that tortures us and destroys our health
and life comes from nowhere but our bodies themselves. They are born in
the nature of disease. To quote the great master Aryadeva:

> The human body is nothing more than the composition of the
> four elements: fire, water, earth, and air. By nature opposing forces,
> they are like four violent snakes being kept in one container. The
> four elements in our bodies always fight against each other. When-
> ever there is an imbalance between them physical illness is the
> result.

We feel strong and healthy when the elements within our bodies are in a
temporary state of balance. This physical balance is very fragile and our
health depends completely on it. Even a slight change in the process of the
elemental circulation within our bodies, or environmental change, can
cause an imbalance. So, although we may feel healthy now we should
remember the words of Geshe Potowa Rinpoche:

> Since birth we have been facing the disease that will cause our even-
> tual death. Thus we cannot rely on this fragile corpse. Practice pure
> Dharma and free yourself from the suffering of rebirth.

3 & 4. The Suffering of Old Age and Death

The suffering of old age is an inescapable fear that all human beings have to face. From the moment we enter our mother's womb we approach old age and death; every second brings us closer. No sooner have we grown up than our youthful bodies begin to be destroyed by the suffering of old age. Beautiful or attractive faces turn to ugly ones, full of wrinkles. Our teeth fall out. Shining eyes fade and fall deep into their sockets. Flexible bodies become stiff, bent, and incontinent, and we lose control over our physical and mental coordination. Our memory begins to decline and we become like a living corpse, awaiting death. Buddha says:

> When we fall into the suffering of old age, our physical strength collapses like a beautiful tree being destroyed by a storm. Our body becomes rotten like a beautiful town turned into a dirty ruin. Youthful, attractive men and women dry out like a lovely forest of Jain-den trees devastated by fire. The suffering of old age will take away all our physical and mental strengths leaving us powerless, as if we were sinking into a deep mire. Old age brings constant pain and carries us mercilessly toward death. Having realized this unbearable suffering we should try to release ourselves from the bonds of cyclic existence.

Kadampa Geshe Chen Ngawa says:

> The suffering of death is considered to be severe but short. For me the suffering of old age is even worse.

Similarly Karmapa Rinpoche says:

> Since the suffering of old age descends upon us gradually, we do not notice that we have been undergoing this suffering since our birth. If the suffering of old age came upon us suddenly, it would be unbearable for us.

*5 & 6. The Suffering of Constantly Facing Undesirable Things and
Being Separated from Desirable Ones*

Not only are we humans subject to the four sufferings of birth, sickness, old age, and death, but we constantly have to endure endless undesirable things, such as meeting people whom we don't like and who cause us trouble. We have to face criticism, complaints, and rude or harsh words. Then there are those who disregard us, resent us, or even betray us. No matter where we are born the world is full of endless sadness and sorrows, of wars, diseases, poverty, and starvation. We ourselves are also subject to these undesirable things and are often caught in this suffering. There is no way to escape from it: we are born in the nature of such suffering.

We are also tormented by the fear of losing desirable things and always have to face being separated from beloved friends and relatives. As a result we experience unbearable sorrow and pain. There is also the constant fear of losing the youthful beauty of our bodies and of losing our fame and wealth. Here the great master Aryadeva says:

> In the human realm the rich always suffer mentally and the poor suffer physically. Human beings' happiness is destroyed by these two sufferings. Furthermore, all those who are born into the human realm always suffer from dissatisfaction, no matter how much they gain their heart's desire. When they fail to get what they want, they are discouraged and their hearts are filled with sorrow. Therefore they can never rest in true peace and happiness.

Not one of us wants to be separated from those we love so much. Whenever we have to part from them we experience uncontrollable sorrow and sadness. Likewise we do not want those who feel resentment or hatred toward us to be anywhere near us. However, those whom we have loved often become our enemies—this is totally beyond our control. Thus, we constantly feel anxious and insecure about our relationships with friends and relatives. In the sutra called *Request by the Bodhisattva Pung Zang* Buddha says:

> Our beloved friend often becomes our bitter enemy and our bitter enemy can also become our friend. Both friend and enemy can

change. Strangers also often become our friends or enemies. Realizing these uncertainties we should turn our mind away from being attached to those we like and feeling aversion toward those we dislike. Then we should place our mind on virtuous practice.

7. The Suffering of Not Fulfilling Our Desire

One of the worst sufferings that we human beings face is dissatisfaction. To quote Nagarjuna:

> We are like lepers who gain a little pleasure by warming their bodies in front of a fire: the more they do so, the more their desire for it increases. Thus there is no satisfaction but more and more suffering. We should know that through our desire for pleasure in cyclic existence we suffer in exactly the same way.

If we think about our past lives we will see that from beginningless time we have been born countless times as human beings, gods, animals, hungry ghosts, and hell beings. There is not one kind of rebirth we have not taken, not one place or realm we have not been born into. Thus there is not any kind of pleasure we have not experienced. Likewise there are no sorrows or sufferings we have not undergone. No matter how many pleasures we have gained or how great they have been, we can hardly ever be satisfied with what we have unless we manage to control our insatiable desire. Buddha says in the Vinaya, the teachings on monastic discipline:

> The amount of molten iron we were forced to swallow as hell beings would be much greater than the greatest ocean on earth if it remained and could be piled into a great heap. The amount of heads that our enemies cut off our bodies while fighting during past lives would be greater than Mount Meru if they remained and could be piled into a heap. The amount of water coming from the tears we shed while weeping over the separation from our loved ones and friends would be much greater than the earth's vast oceans, if they remained.

Therefore there is no greater suffering than being discontented. This is what constantly torments us.

8. The Suffering of Being Bound by the Chains of the Suffering Nature of the Five Aggregates

Life in cyclic existence is in the nature of suffering in the sense that under the force of delusion and karma, wherever we are born, whatever kind of body we take, it remains subject to change: birth, growth, old age, death, and rebirth.

When we take rebirth our life is trapped through the bondage of the five aggregates: our body, sensations, cognition, compositional factors, and consciousness (see pages 206–09). If we examine these we will see that each is subject to the chain of cause and conditions. In short, our existence is completely governed by karmic forces and delusion.

Therefore there is no certainty about any pleasures, wealth, or higher rebirths we may gain. The suffering of uncertainty pervades all of cyclic existence.

The Suffering of Uncertainty

Not only do we suffer from not being able to control our desire and attachment, but we can never be certain about anything. Whatever realm we may find ourselves in and however high it may be, it will end and we do not know where we will be reborn. Everything in samsara is totally subject to karmic causes and conditions. The pleasures and positions we find can only last as long as their causes remain. Karmic causes themselves are also transient and once they are finished the results will cease. Therefore all pleasures, prosperity, and positions within samsara are only transient. Here Nagarjuna says:

Having been born as Brahma who dominates the three realms, worthy of the whole world's veneration, we fall back again to this earth through the force of our karma. Having been born as a Sakravarten king who dominates the whole earth, we are born again as the poorest of the poor. Having had a lifetime of pleasure, fondling the breasts and hips of celestial maidens, we again fall back into the hell realms to face the unbearable suffering of having our body crushed and slashed. Having had the long enjoyment of dwelling on the soft and springy grassland of Mount Meru, we again fall back into hell, to undergo the terrible suffering in the land of red-hot cinders and the suffering of sinking into a swamp of filth for a very long time. Having had the long pleasure of playing with many attractive celestial friends in beautiful gardens, we again return to hell to have the limbs of our body cut with very sharp sword-like leaves while traveling through forests of iron trees. Having had the delight and pleasure of enjoying ourselves with beautiful girls and boys, swimming in sparkling clear pools adorned with golden lotuses, we fall again into the caustic and boiling waters of endless rebirth in the hell realms. Having achieved the great pleasures of the celestial realms and even the great bliss of non-attachment to being born in the Brahma realm, again we face unimaginable suffering from being the fuel of the terrible ceaseless fires of hell.

If we were to see how many rebirths we have taken, we would be heartbroken. Nagarjuna says:

The amount of bones from all the previous bodies that we have been reborn in would be greater than Mount Meru, if they remained and could be piled in a heap.

We are still in the same position. Unless we realize how fortunate we are to have found the precious human rebirth and practice Dharma purely, we will have to face the unimaginable and immeasurable suffering of taking countless rebirths.

This precious body that we have now will soon be lost. When we depart from this life and go to the next, no one can travel with us to help us. Realizing this, we should try not to waste the extremely rare opportunity we have as human beings.

Meditation on the Suffering Nature
of Cyclic Existence

I am extremely fortunate to have found this precious human rebirth. It not only provides me with the incredible opportunities to be able to achieve even enlightenment in a short time, but is also my only chance to see how mindless I would be if I were to waste such opportunities. I shall not waste my time by indulging in the little pleasures I gain through having this precious human rebirth.

If I remain careless about my true happiness and am not aware of the impermanent nature of samsaric life, then soon, when death descends on me, I will feel so much regret. I will fall back into the bottomless suffering of the lower realms: the animals, hungry ghosts, and hell beings.

Once born in the lower realms it is very difficult to be reborn in the higher realms again. And even if I take rebirth in one of the higher realms, there is still no security in whatever pleasures I would gain. No matter how high a rebirth I might gain, even as Brahma or Indra, unless I am able to overcome my delusions, I will always remain liable to fall back into the misery of the lower realms. Thus there is no certainty whatsoever in the pleasures of cyclic existence.

Even when I am reborn in the higher realms I will be bound to undergo inescapable sufferings, such as the suffering of birth, sickness, old age, and death; the suffering of constantly facing undesirable things; the suffering of being separated from desirable things; the suffering of not fulfilling my desire; and the suffering of being bound by the chains of the suffering nature of the five aggregates.

No matter how many samsaric pleasures I have gained from being born as the king of the gods, there is no satisfaction. Thus I will always suffer from dissatisfaction. Although I love my dear ones and cannot bear to be separated from them even for a short time, there are no certainties about my relationships with people in samsara. Best friends often change to become bitter enemies. And although we feel hatred toward those people who cause us trouble, even our worst enemy often becomes our best friend.

When I was born I was alone and when I depart from this life to go to the next, no one can come and help me. I have to travel alone, leaving everything behind, at the mercy of whatever karma I have accumulated. I should not waste this precious opportunity and should try my best to keep on the right path that can lead me to liberation from the confused state of cyclic existence.

O my Guru Buddha Shakyamuni, please bestow the blessings of your great compassion, love, and power on me so that I may gain realizations of the suffering nature of cyclic existence and thus be able to benefit all mother beings.

After reflecting on the suffering nature of cyclic existence as explained above, recite the following passage from *The Instructions of the Vinaya Sutra*:

O friend, you should know that cyclic existence is in the nature of suffering.

From ignorance arises the force of karma.

From the karmic force arises the force of the stream of consciousness, which carries us toward the next rebirth.

Depending on the force of consciousness arises the stage of name and form.

From the stage of name and form arise the sense faculties.

From the sense faculties arises the stage of contact with external objects.

From contact arises sensation.

Depending on sensation arise desire and attachment.

From desire and attachment arises clinging to transitory pleasure.

From clinging arises ripening karma.

From ripening karma comes rebirth again.

From rebirth arises the suffering of old age and death.

Furthermore beings in cyclic existence are tormented by the suffering of meeting with undesirable things, losing desirable things, and not fulfilling their desire; thus they feel endless sorrow and wail on account of their unbearable suffering.

O friend, rebirth in samsara is in the nature of suffering.

Having realized this we should eliminate our ignorance. When the origin of ignorance is extinguished there is no longer the force of karma.

Once the origin of the force of karma is extinguished there is no

longer the force of the stream of consciousness to carry us toward
the next rebirth.

When the origin of the force of the stream of consciousness is
extinguished there is no longer the stage of name and form.

When the origin of the stage of name and form is extinguished
there is no longer the occurrence of the sense organs.

When the origin of the sense organs is extinguished there is no
longer desire and attachment.

When the origin of desire and attachment is extinguished there
is no longer clinging to transitory pleasure.

When the origin of clinging to transitory pleasure is extinguished there is no longer any ripening karma.

When the origin of ripening karma is extinguished there is no
longer rebirth.

When the origin of rebirth is extinguished there is no longer the
suffering of old age and death.

Thus the suffering of meeting with undesirable objects, the suffering of losing desirable objects, the suffering of not fulfilling our
desire, and the suffering of sorrow, unbearable grief, and wailing—
all sufferings are extinguished.

O friend, this is the complete extinction of cyclic existence. You
then transcend the misery of cyclic existence. This is the highest
happiness, the ultimate liberation, completely wholesome, everlasting peace.

Having recited this, visualize that white light comes from the place
between the eyebrows of the buddhas and bodhisattvas in the merit field
and dissolves into the place between your eyebrows, filling your body
with white light and dispersing all the negative actions you have done
through your body.

Then red light comes from the throat chakra of all the buddhas and
bodhisattvas, dissolves into your throat chakra, and fills your body with red
light, purifying all your negative actions of speech.

Finally blue light comes from the heart chakra of all the buddhas and
bodhisattvas and dissolves into your heart chakra, filling your body with
blue light and purifying all your previous negative mental attitudes.

PART FOUR

*Meditations on the High Level of
Inner Development*

Atisha

10. Encouraging Ourselves to Develop Bodhicitta, the Mind of Enlightenment

Through practicing the right path leading to complete liberation from the suffering of cyclic existence, we will be able to go beyond its confused state and will find everlasting peace of mind.

If we are wise enough, however, we will realize that it is not sufficient to gain mere freedom from cyclic existence. Although we will never fall back into it, we will not yet have abandoned the subtle imprints of delusion and will thus be deprived of the higher qualities that Enlightened Ones possess. Buddhas always encourage arhats, who have freed themselves from the cycle of rebirth, to enter into the practice of the Mahayana or great compassion so that they can achieve the enlightened state. Also we can clearly see that unless we are heartless, it is not appropriate for us to be concerned only with our own rescue, abandoning all our mother beings who suffer endlessly under the same conditions in cyclic existence. Buddha says in the short *Perfection of Wisdom Sutra*:

> When those who have the seed of the bodhimind, the mind aspiring to enlightenment, see their mother beings wandering on the dangerous, endless mountain cliff of cyclic existence with no wisdom eye, how can they bear to abandon them in this extremely piteous situation? Of course they would selflessly jump to rescue them from this unimaginable danger. This is the nature of bodhiminded beings.

Similarly, Nagarjuna says in his *Letter to a Friend*:

Even stupid animals such as cows know how to rescue themselves from suffering; they know how to get water when they suffer from thirst; they know how to get fresh new shoots when they suffer from hunger. Thus, being concerned about our own suffering is not the Wise Ones' way of thinking. Bodhisattvas always neglect their own happiness and wisely concern themselves with the benefit of countless other beings. This is their great significant quality. Through this, Wise Ones are not only able to accomplish their own highest happiness, but are also able to fulfill the needs of countless other beings.

We can therefore feel great joy at having this very rare opportunity to meet the stainless living teachings on great compassion. And we should sincerely practice the great vehicle of the bodhisattvas, the Mahayana Path, through which many wise beings have reached the enlightened state and many more will travel toward it.

All our mother beings remain powerlessly drowning in the ageless ocean of cyclic existence. However, we ourselves are now in a good position to be able to benefit them. It is not only our duty to help them, but we are actually their only hope. If we neglect them we would be mindless. There is no greater shame than this; there is no greater deceit than this.

The Benefits of Generating Bodhicitta

Buddha says in many sutras:

The only seed from which enlightenment arises is bodhicitta, the sympathetic attitude sincerely benefiting others and wishing to liberate them. Just as the crescent moon is more worthy of veneration than the full moon, so even buddhas venerate those who newly generate bodhicitta. They show more concern toward them than toward the more advanced bodhisattvas. It is the same when people grow medicinal plants: they take more care of them when they are still seedlings and so the seedlings grow strong.

It is also said in many sutras that buddhas have so much respect for bodhisattvas that they are even willing to serve them and draw their chariots when they travel.

The benefits gained from generating great sympathy, wishing to liberate other beings, are measureless. If we truly do not want unhappiness, then we must purify the negative actions we have done in the past, for all suffering comes from nowhere but previous unwholesome karma. None of us want suffering, but there is no way at all we can avoid facing undesirable things, unless the cause of unhappiness is purified. Bodhicitta is the most powerful way to purify negative karma. Shantideva says:

> We have been accumulating immeasurable, powerful non-virtuous karma since beginningless time. This cannot be purified by any virtuous practice other than bodhicitta.

Similarly, Buddha himself says in the sutras:

> Bodhicitta is such a powerful virtue, that generating it even for one moment can cleanse our mind of the enormous amount of non-virtuous karma accumulated over many eons. Thus there is no greater virtue than generating bodhicitta.

Lama Tsonghkapa said:

> Although bodhisattvas sincerely want to take sufferings upon themselves, instead of experiencing suffering they hardly come across any undesirable things. They always have a happy life because of their practice of bodhicitta.

Kadampa Geshe Chen Ngawa, who was a great practitioner of bodhicitta, always sincerely prayed that as soon as he passed away he would be reborn in hell for the sake of the beings there. When he was about to die many signs occurred, showing that he would be reborn in a pure land. This made him unhappy. He asked one of his disciples to arrange extensive offerings and requested all the buddhas and bodhisattvas to grant his wish. But as soon as he passed away he was born in the pure land of Avalokiteshvara.

Furthermore, it is said in many sutras that the merit gained from developing bodhicitta can yield ceaseless results from the moment we generate it until we become enlightened. But the results gained from developing all other virtues will cease when they have been experienced once. When we have generated bodhicitta, however, all other virtues become the pure cause of enlightenment. No matter how much extensive knowledge, profound wisdom, or miraculous power we may have, none of these will help us attain enlightenment unless they are nourished by bodhicitta. Here Shantideva said:

> Just as special elixirs can transform base metals into gold, once we have generated bodhicitta even our impure body can gradually be transformed into the peerless jewel of the Rupakaya, the Buddha's body.

Although arhats are endowed with many miraculous powers, incredible wisdom, and stable concentration, buddhas still do not accept them as their Sons or Daughters. However, if we generate bodhicitta, regardless of whether we have much knowledge or not, we are immediately held in esteem by the buddhas as their private Son or Daughter. The great Tsonghkapa said:

> You may be born as an animal, but if you generate bodhicitta, you still become worthy of veneration, even by Buddha. No matter how many high or profound qualities you may have, you have not entered the Mahayana Path until you have generated this precious mind of bodhicitta.

Similarly, Shantideva said:

> Even though you are locked in the prison of cyclic existence and find yourself in a piteous situation, if you generate bodhicitta you immediately gain the title of the Son or Daughter of the Tathagata and are born into the family of Buddha.

Buddha says in the sutra called *The Life Story of Maitreya Buddha*:

O friend, a broken diamond surpasses all other precious jewels, even the most beautiful golden ornaments. Although it is a fragment, it still retains the title of the greatest precious jewel and can take away all poverty.

O friend, in the same way, as soon as you generate bodhicitta, even though you may not have other virtuous qualities, you surpass even Sravaka arhats and Pratyeka buddhas who possess many incredible qualities and you still deserve the title of a Son or Daughter of Buddha. Thus you can liberate other beings from endless suffering.

Bodhicitta is essential for gaining realizations on the path. Once Atisha was asked why it was that not many practitioners in Tibet were able to achieve any spiritual progress on the path, even though they practiced the most profound highest yoga tantra. Atisha smiled and said:

Everyone has some kind of deity to whom they are devoted and some kind of tantric mantra to recite, but what they lack is great compassion, the true motivation of the Mahayana.

When Atisha asked some Tibetan yogis about their main practices, some of them named their highest tantric deities such as Guhyasamaja, Heruka, or Hevajra. He was not happy with their answers and said, "It is sad. It is a pity that the yogis have become rotten."

While Atisha was in his monastery in India he studied many sutras and tantras and became a great scholar. After he had become very well-known he saw some dakinis in a vision and they advised him to go to Bodhgaya soon. There he would meet an emanation of Tara who would prophesy where he would find the great teacher of bodhicitta. So he traveled to Bodhgaya and Tara advised him to meet the great Lama Serlingpa and take the full teachings on bodhicitta from him. Then he should consolidate all his practices in the practice of bodhicitta. So Atisha went to Indonesia and spent twelve years there, taking the teachings from Lama Serlingpa. He himself said, "Although I have taken many profound teachings on sutra and tantra, the bodhicitta teachings are of most benefit to me." And he would advise anybody who came to him to practice compassion and love.

Lama Tsonghkapa said:

> No matter how much highest tantra we may practice, it will all
> remain as mere words or imagination and we will not gain a true
> experience of tantra until we are able to cultivate the most sympa-
> thetic attitude of having great compassion for all mother beings.

If we single-pointedly practice great compassion, then, with little effort, we
will be able to gain all other virtues at both sutra and tantra levels. But if
we neglect the practice of compassion, we can hardly gain any true experience on any path, no matter how many profound practices we do and
how much effort we make. Therefore all the great practitioners such as
Atisha and Tsonghkapa single-pointedly concentrated on the practice of
bodhicitta or compassion. In the sutra called *The Collection of Pure Dharma*
Buddha says:

> There is no need for bodhisattvas to engage in many different prac-
> tices. Rather they should consolidate themselves in one practice:
> that of compassion. If a bodhisattva accomplishes true great com-
> passion, all other excellent qualities are automatically achieved, for
> it is great compassion that passes on all Buddha's immeasurable
> qualities. Just as all the subjects of a Chakravartin king gather wher-
> ever he dwells or stays, likewise, all the great qualities of the buddhas
> are automatically present in those who accomplish great compas-
> sion. And in the same way that all the organs of a body can func-
> tion as long as the life-force is strong, so, if you generate great
> compassion, all other virtuous qualities automatically arise. Thus
> we gain enlightenment quickly.

Therefore it is essential for us to follow the instructions given by the great
Mahayana yogis on how to develop the true experience of the Mahayana
Path. Otherwise we will be forever jumping at anything that sounds more
interesting or more profound and spend a whole lifetime wandering from
one practice to another without achieving any concrete experience.

Kadampa lamas always advise us that we should really look hard for the
source of the marvelous qualities of a bodhisattva. Once we have found the

origin, we should then consolidate the practice if we truly wish to attain those high qualities. To quote Chandrakirti:

> When we first generate bodhicitta, compassion is as important as the seed is to the growth of the crop. During the course of our practice of the Mahayana Path, while developing realizations, compassion is as important as water in the soil is for the ripening crop. Finally, when enlightenment is achieved, fulfilling the needs of all beings, compassion is likened to the fully ripened crop.

Thus bodhicitta is the only source of all happiness both for ourselves and others. It is the great medicine that cures the illness of all kinds of suffering. It is the only path along which all buddhas have traveled to reach enlightenment. It gives us incredible skills with which we can automatically fulfill our own goal—only by sacrificing our own happiness in order to benefit others. Tsonghkapa says:

> Bodhicitta not only enables us to ascend from a happy state to the happiest state, but also enables us to disperse the suffering of countless beings. This is the essence of the Bodhisattva Path.

11. How to Develop Bodhicitta

Maitreya says in *The Ornament for Clear Realization*:

> To generate bodhicitta means to develop the sincere aspiration to attain enlightenment for the sake of others.

It is almost impossible to develop such an aspiration sincerely, unless we feel great sympathy toward others—so great that we cannot bear to see them suffer endlessly in cyclic existence.

As we discussed earlier, to rescue ourselves from the suffering of cyclic existence, we do not need to take on the great task of practicing the Mahayana Path. We can easily attain our own everlasting peace through practicing the Hinayana Path. But bodhisattvas clearly see that it is not appropriate to try and rescue only themselves, without any concern for the piteous situation of all mother beings, who suffer equally in cyclic existence.

When we examine how we can truly help all mother beings to be liberated from the suffering of cyclic existence, we will realize that at the moment we do not have the ability to help even one single sentient being to be free. Even the Hinayana arhats, who have completely reached beyond cyclic existence, have no such power. Only Buddha can fulfill this task. Therefore, unless we achieve such a state, we will not be able to fulfill our wish to liberate all mother beings from cyclic existence. Thus, the unshakable, sincere aspiration to become enlightened for the sake of all others arises from great compassion toward them.

Bodhicitta, therefore, is the strong determination to commit ourselves completely to attaining enlightenment so that all other sentient beings can be liberated from the unbearable sufferings of cyclic existence. Regardless of any hardship we have to face, regardless of how long it takes us to achieve the enlightened state, we remain true to this selfless aspiration. But this incredible aspiration only arises when we see the suffering of others very deeply and cannot bear to leave them any longer in such endless, miserable conditions. Nagarjuna says, "The root of bodhicitta is great compassion."

In the Mahayana tradition two ways of developing bodhicitta are taught: (1) through the six causes and (2) through exchanging ourself with others. Both were taught by Buddha Shakyamuni and descended from him in an unbroken lineage to the present-day lineage-holders. The system of the six causes was transmitted by Buddha to his chief disciple, the great bodhisattva Maitreya. The system of exchanging ourself with others was transmitted to the great bodhisattva Manjushri.

Atisha fully received the teachings of these two systems from many outstanding Mahayana masters, particularly from his two distinguished bodhicitta teachers, Dharmarakshita and Lama Serlingpa. He then brought this living tradition to Tibet where it was passed on until it reached Tsonghkapa, who combined the two systems and taught a unique and very effective way of generating bodhicitta.

Here we will learn how to develop bodhicitta according to the living tradition of Tsonghkapa. He says:

No matter how much effort we make when meditating on bodhicitta, our practice will remain as mere words until we develop great compassion and a loving mind toward all beings equally. Once we feel as compassionate and loving toward all sentient beings as we do toward our dearest, beloved ones, then we will automatically and enthusiastically be able to help them with whatever difficulties they have. Thus bodhicitta arises from compassion.

The key practice is therefore to develop a loving mind equally toward all beings. Both systems of generating bodhicitta focus on developing this loving mind. The first system of the six causes shows us how to develop a sincere feeling of tenderness toward all beings through seeing that they have all been equally kind to us. The six causes are: (1) recognition of all beings as our mothers; (2) remembering their kindness; (3) meditation on repaying their kindness; (4) meditation on great love; (5) great compassion; and (6) special sympathy.

The second system of exchanging ourself with others shows how we can develop loving kindness toward all others by seeing that cherishing our own happiness is the source of our suffering and that cherishing other beings is the source of all happiness both for ourselves and others. There are four stages in the meditation on exchanging ourself with others: (1) reflecting on the disadvantages of cherishing ourself and the advantages of cherishing others; (2) equalizing ourself with others; (3) the actual way of exchanging ourself with others; (4) meditation on giving our own happiness to others and taking their suffering upon ourself.

In the combined system of developing bodhicitta we are led to meditate on equanimity as the foundation, and then to the first two of the six causes. Meditation on the four remaining causes comes within the practice of exchanging ourself with others, so these do not form separate meditations. Atisha says:

> The practice of bodhicitta is nothing but letting go of the feeling of indifference toward others and maintaining a sincere and loving mind toward all—whoever we meet, see, or live with.

The foundation for developing such a loving mind is equanimity. At present we often feel resentment toward those who cause us trouble or we dislike people for some reason. We feel attached to those who benefit us at the moment or whom we like for some reason. We have no particular feelings for those who do not benefit us or whom we neither like nor dislike. There is no doubt that when we gain a loving attitude toward others equally, whether they trouble us, help us, or do neither, we ourselves can always remain happy—not to mention how much we will be able to help others. Kadampa Lama Ahrme Renchen said:

> Now I am very happy because of my little experience of loving kindness toward other beings. This little experience is due to the

kindness of those beings who trouble or harm me. I must feel grateful toward them and regard them as my teachers.

Most of the unhappiness that we experience in our daily lives is due to our lack of equanimity toward others. Thus, in the practice of developing bodhicitta, we are first led to the meditation on developing equanimity.

Since beginningless time, our minds have been fooled by the temptation of being attached to those we like and feeling hatred toward those we dislike. As a result of these negative states of mind, not only do we cause endless suffering to others, but we also bring endless unhappiness to ourselves. Most of the unhappiness that we experience in daily life arises from these negative states of mind.

Buddha says:

Those who at present temporarily hold a hostile attitude toward us have been our beloved mother, father, friend, brother, and sister countless times. Those who benefit us now have also been our bitter enemy. Therefore, we should cast away any kind of resentment toward those who harm us, cast away attachment to those we like, and thus extend a loving mind toward all beings equally.

If we examine this closely, those whom we regard as our enemy have been our dear mother and friend countless times, and the amount of tears we wept when we were separated from them then would be much greater than the deepest ocean on earth if they remained. Likewise, those whom we are attached to and cannot bear to be separated from, even for a while, have been our bitter enemy countless times. If our own corpses, which our present friends killed when they were our enemies in past lives, were piled up, the heap would be much greater than Mount Meru.

There is no certainty about our relationships with others. Friends become enemies, enemies often change to become friends. If we closely check up on why we feel resentment toward those we regard as our enemy, the only reason is because they harm us or cause us trouble. When they cause us trouble, their minds are completely overpowered by delusion. In the same way, when they are overpowered by negative thoughts they harm others or even kill themselves. So, if we are wise, we will realize that it would be more appropriate to feel compassion for them instead of hatred, to help them free their minds from the influence of negative thought.

Since beginningless time we have harbored resentment toward anybody who has caused us trouble and have become attached to those who have benefited us. What have we gained from this? We have accumulated nothing but immeasurable non-virtuous karma. As a result we have even been born in the worst hell, again and again.

But now, only this once, we have fortunately gained the precious human rebirth through which we can even achieve the enlightened state in one lifetime. If we still allow ourselves to remain carelessly under the influence of these non-virtuous thoughts, we will again experience the immeasurable suffering of being born in the lower realms when we depart from this life. How mindless we would be! Here Shantideva says:

> Those to whom we are attached will soon be separated from us, as will those toward whom we feel hatred. When death comes nobody can travel with us, yet the non-virtues, which we have been accumulating through attachment and hatred, will follow us and as a result we will experience unimaginable suffering.

Tsonghkapa says:

> From our point of view, all beings are equal to us because they have all been our beloved mother, father, brother, sister, and friend countless times. From their point of view, all beings should also be treated as equal to us because they equally desire happiness and shun unhappiness. Therefore, we should try to maintain a loving mind toward all beings equally.

Before doing the following meditations, we should do the prerequisite practices as presented on pages 35–56.

Meditation on Equanimity

Since beginningless time my mind has been tempted by the evil influence of partiality toward my fellow beings, of attachment to those who temporarily benefit me, and of hatred toward those whom I regard as my enemy. Under the temptation of such harmful states of mind, I have accumulated an immeasurable amount of non-virtuous karma. As a result of this I have undergone unimaginable suffering by being reborn in the lower realms for countless eons. Even though I have received such a happy, precious rebirth, these troublesome thoughts never allow me to rest in peace. If I look closely, I can trace most of the unhappiness that I experience in this life to these harmful thoughts of partiality. Moreover, if I do not recognize how much suffering this has brought me and carelessly allow my mind to remain under the influence of this temptation, how mindless I would be.

If I examine why I hate those who cause me trouble, I will realize that it is because I think they cause me suffering. This thought is based on a totally false view—how can I rely on it? Whatever suffering I experience is not the creation of my fellow beings, but is the manifestation of my non-virtuous karma. Why should I therefore feel hatred toward them? I should feel pity for them instead, because they are powerlessly governed by the force of their own non-virtuous karma.

From my point of view, I should treat them all equally, because those whom I dislike at present have also been my dearest friends countless times. And those to whom I am attached have also been my bitter enemies. From their point of view, they all equally desire happiness and shun unhappiness.

O my Guru Buddha Shakyamuni, please bestow the blessing of your compassion and wisdom on me so that I may gain the realization of equanimity toward all my fellow beings.

Now follows the meditation on the first of the six causes:

Meditation on the Recognition of All Beings as Our Mothers

Mothers naturally always have a strong feeling of love for their children, no matter whether they are humans or animals. When I honestly think of how much kindness my mother has given me, I naturally feel strong love for her. She always thinks of me as her only child.

There is not a single sentient being who has not been my mother. If I examine the fact that I have been born in cyclic existence since beginningless time, I will see that there is not one kind of place left where I have not taken rebirth and there is not one kind of rebirth that I have not taken. The number of times that each and every sentient being has been my mother is beyond estimation. The only reason why I do not have the same feeling toward others as I do toward my mother of this life is that I do not remember my past lives, when they were my mothers; but they were still my mothers.

How can I discriminate between the one who became my mother in this life and those who were my mothers in previous lives? For me there is no difference between the mother who brought me up in this life and the mothers who brought me up in previous lives. Thus, I should regard all beings as my mother and should maintain a loving mind toward them all, as I do toward my present mother.

O my Guru Buddha Shakyamuni, please bestow the blessing of your great kindness and wisdom on me so that I may achieve the realization that all beings are my mothers.

Now follows the meditation on the second of the six causes:

Meditation on Remembering the Kindness of All Beings

The kindness that I have received from my mother, even within this life, is incredible, if I honestly open my mind toward it. It is natural for mothers to always think of the happiness of their children. When their child is born, mothers feel even happier than if they had found a priceless, precious jewel. They totally sacrifice their lives to the care of their children. They experience much more sorrow when they find their child even a little unwell than if they were seriously sick themselves. They experience extreme happiness whenever they find their child is happy, even when they themselves are not well.

When I was a child, I was helplessly dependent on my mother. Let me imagine how I would be now if she had neglected me then. I was not even

able to distinguish between poison and proper food. My mother totally sacrificed her life to protect me from every danger and provided me with all
that was necessary to nourish me and bring me up. She did this in every
possible way, according to her ability. I owe all the happiness I have at
present to her. Even as I was growing up, she was always concerned with
my education and livelihood.

I received the same kindness from all sentient beings when they became
my mother. They sacrificed their whole lives and energy to my happiness.
I should always remind myself of the incredible kindness I have received
from sentient beings, who have all been my dear mother.

*O my Guru Buddha Shakyamuni, please bestow your kindness and wisdom
on me so that I may always remember the kindness of all sentient beings, my
mothers.*

After reflecting in this way, visualize yourself surrounded by all your
mother sentient beings.

From the hearts of all the buddhas and bodhisattvas in the merit field
white light radiates together with nectar, entering the heart of each and
every sentient being, purifying all their contaminated karma and delusions, and filling their bodies with pure nectar.

Firmly believe that all mother beings have been freed from all their suffering together with its causes, and that they have achieved everlasting
happiness.

Having meditated on the first two causes we now combine the two systems
of generating bodhicitta. As mentioned earlier, the remaining four causes
(meditation on repaying the kindness of our mothers; meditation on great
love, great compassion, and special sympathy) are contained within the
practice of exchanging ourself with others. To remind ourselves, this has
four stages: (1) reflecting on the disadvantages of cherishing ourself and the
advantages of cherishing others; (2) equalizing ourself with others; (3) the
actual way of exchanging ourself with others; (4) meditation on giving our
own happiness to others and taking their suffering upon ourself.

In order to accomplish any practice, it is utterly important to have great
enthusiasm, otherwise we will not be able to fulfill our task, however much

effort we make. It is through our enthusiasm that we can joyfully practice whatever path we follow without having a sense of difficulty or hardship. Therefore, when we enter into the practice of exchanging ourself with others, we should first reflect on the disadvantages of cherishing ourself and the advantages of cherishing others. Once we see how cherishing ourself brings suffering to us and how cherishing others brings happiness to us, we then automatically become eager to practice exchanging ourself with others.

1. The Disadvantages of Cherishing Ourself and the Advantages of Cherishing Others

Buddha says:

> All the sufferings and evils in the world arise from nowhere else but the evil thought of cherishing ourself.

If we look closely, we can see very clearly how all unhappiness and troubles originate from the evil mind of self-cherishing. All the fears that we experience, all the conflicts in families and between nations, any unhappy situations whatsoever are caused by nothing else but this evil thought. Shantideva says:

> That which brings all evil and causes all unhappiness is the demon of the self-cherishing mind. How can we remain happy if we allow this demon to dwell in our hearts?

Thus, if we truly want happiness, we should try to destroy the evil of the self-cherishing mind. There is no way for us to find stable happiness and peace as long as our minds remain subject to this evil thought.

We always fear our enemies, evil spirits, and disease, but they are nothing compared to the inner evil of the self-cherishing mind. However cruel our enemies may be, they cannot take away any of our inner virtuous qualities, nor can they throw us into a lower rebirth. Moreover, all the sufferings that we experience in this life, not to mention those we experience in the lower realms, are the result of the negative actions that we have accumulated under the influence of the self-cherishing mind. Therefore Atisha says:

We should place the blame for all our troubles and suffering on nothing else but our own self-cherishing attitude, and we should always remind ourselves of the kindness we receive from others. If we practice this, not only do we ourselves become truly happy, but there is no end to the happiness we can give others.

Similarly, Kadampa Geshe Chen Ngawa says:

When we are sick, nothing else causes our sickness but the self-cherishing mind. When we face the suffering of old age, nothing else makes us old but our self-cherishing mind, taking away all our physical strength and beauty. When we lose our wealth, it is not actually a thief or robber that takes it away, but our self-cherishing mind robs us of it. When we die, no evil spirit takes away our life, but the evil thought of self-cherishing kills us.

Thus, there is no evil spirit or enemy that can harm us as much as this inner demon of the self-cherishing mind. Since beginningless time it has brought us endless suffering impelling us into the unbearable fires of the hot hells and bitterly icy lands of the cold hells. In the guise of being dear to us, it always fools us. It is easier to recognize our external enemies when they come to harm us because they usually come with fierce and angry faces. But the inner demon of the self-cherishing mind always appears in a tempting way and is therefore very difficult to recognize.

Shantideva says:

However cruel the external evils may be, if we surrender ourselves to them sincerely, they will become friendly toward us and even help us. But if we try to become friendly with the demon of the self-cherishing mind, it will harm us more! Therefore it is absolutely wrong if we allow our minds to remain under the influence of this evil thought. Why should we not fight against it?

We cannot imagine the harm this self-cherishing mind has brought to us since beginningless time. Now we are so fortunate to have attained the precious human rebirth and to have met with the pure Mahayana teachings of Lord Buddha. Through these we have the wisdom to discriminate deeply between the cause of suffering and the cause of happiness. However, if we remain careless and do not try to destroy the self-cherishing mind and do not develop great love toward others while we have this precious opportunity, then sooner or later death will come and this inner evil will again throw us into the unbearable sufferings of hell.

Buddha says, "All the happiness that exists in the world arises from cherishing other beings." If we have a cherishing attitude toward others, then no matter whom we are with, we can always remain happy. The mind of cherishing others not only gives tremendous happiness to those we happen to be with, it also enables us to face any difficulties, hardships, or unhappy situations. Whatever happiness we have now or will experience is the result of cherishing others. Shantideva says:

> It is needless to say much about how cherishing ourself brings suffering and cherishing others brings happiness. If we look at the difference between Enlightened Beings who have only been cherishing others, and the other beings who cherish only themselves, we will be able to see the advantages of cherishing others and the disadvantages of cherishing ourself.

Lama Tsonghkapa says:

> Cherishing ourself is the source of all loss. Cherishing others is the source of all gain.

2. Equalizing Ourself with Others

Under the temptation of the self-cherishing mind, we always cherish ourselves, thinking only of our own happiness, unconcerned with the suffering we may cause others. Through this selfish attitude we have accumulated limitless non-virtuous karma. As a result we have undergone endless suffering since beginningless time. Now we should recognize that others are all equal to us, whether we regard them as enemies, friends, or neutrally. They want happiness and shun unhappiness, just like ourselves.

There is no way for us to be liberated from suffering and gain true happiness unless we are able to subdue this self-cherishing attitude. When we have difficulties—when we are sick, lose a friend or wealth, or have to face bitter criticism—our happy mood suddenly goes and we become unhappy. As others are in exactly the same situation, we should be concerned about their happiness and sorrow just as we are concerned about our own. Just as we have feelings, sensations, and thoughts, so too do all other beings.

To quote the great Tsonghkapa:

> All beings desire happiness and hate unhappiness in the same way we do. Therefore, just as we share sorrows and unhappiness with the members of our own family, so should we share them with all other beings, regardless of their physical differences. This attitude of equalizing ourself with others not only releases us from many difficulties and hardships caused by our own narrow attitudes, it also enables us to feel love toward our fellow beings, whoever we may be with.

3. The Actual Way of Exchanging Ourself with Others

If we truly want to achieve the highest happiness for ourselves and the most effective state through which we will be able to liberate countless beings from the suffering of cyclic existence, then we must be able to exchange ourselves with others. This means to develop an open mind, so that gradually the attitude of cherishing ourself will decrease and we can develop a cherishing and loving mind toward all other beings. We can do this by realizing the fact that the self-cherishing mind is the source of all suffering and that cherishing others is the source of all happiness.

Since beginningless time we have been cherishing only ourselves. What have we gained from this? Nothing but endless suffering. Whatever happiness we have experienced in our past lives, whatever happiness we experience in this life and whatever happiness we will experience in our future lives is only the result of cherishing others. If we are really truthful and sincere with ourselves, shouldn't we be happy to throw out this inner demon of the self-cherishing mind? Why shouldn't we take up this priceless treasure, the precious jewel of the mind cherishing others?

Shantideva says:

> Those who truly wish to protect themselves as well as others from
> the unbearable sufferings of cyclic existence should practice this
> quintessential method of exchanging themselves with others.

It goes without saying that we will not be able to achieve the enlightened
state without getting rid of the evil thought of self-cherishing. We can
hardly remain happy in cyclic existence unless we subdue this negative
mind. Again Shantideva says:

> There are many fears around us, evil spirits, cruel beings, and fear-
> ful enemies. None of them can ever throw us into the suffering of
> a lower rebirth, yet this inner demon of the self-cherishing mind,
> which has been dwelling within our hearts since beginningless time,
> throws us instantly into the fires of the hot hells, which can burn the
> whole world instantaneously.

All the excellent qualities of bodhisattvas and buddhas arise from casting
away the self-cherishing attitude and developing the mind cherishing
others. Therefore, it is essential for us to be able to develop the sincere
attitude of concern for the happiness of other beings. Here Nagarjuna
says:

> If we sincerely practice a loving attitude toward others, even though
> we completely neglect our own happiness, we still automatically
> travel from a happy state to a happier one.

Similarly, the great Tsonghkapa says:

> Loving kindness toward others is the wish-fulfilling tree. It will not
> only fulfill our own happiness, but will also fulfill the needs of
> countless beings. Therefore, the Buddha says that the practice of
> great compassion or love for others is the essence of the whole of
> Buddha's teachings.

It is absolutely incredible to see how much all the buddhas and higher bodhisattvas have benefited the world. Why are they able to do this? For no other reason than through their practice of great compassion and loving kindness to other beings. Shantideva says:

> All the buddhas gathered to discuss what is most beneficial to sentient beings. They all came to agree that bodhicitta is most beneficial.

With great joy, therefore, we should try to subdue the evil of the self-cherishing mind and develop the great loving mind cherishing others in every possible way.

How to Overcome Hindrances to the Practice of Exchanging Ourself with Others

It is said that when we practice exchanging ourself with others, we are often confronted with three major obstacles.

First we find it difficult to get rid of the self-cherishing attitude because we have been conditioned by it since beginningless time. Therefore, whenever we face difficult situations, we can often be tempted into thinking that it might not be possible for us to neglect ourselves completely and truly develop the mind cherishing others.

We must always remember that until we achieve a stable experience of the loving mind, there is always the danger that we might lose courage and confidence in practicing bodhicitta, especially in difficult situations. Kadampa Geshe Chen Ngawa says:

> The hardest thing for the bodhicitta practitioner when confronted with unbearable situations is not to lose courage in practicing the loving mind and compassion. As soon as we face difficulties with others we often forget the conditions of other beings and start to think only of ourselves. Thus we lose the loving mind and instead become anguished and start developing hatred toward others. The important thing is that whenever this happens, we should immediately remember that our mind is being obsessed by the evil demon of the self-cherishing thought.

Thus it is very important to maintain a positive attitude toward the practice of bodhicitta at all times. When we undergo either internal or external difficulties, we should encourage ourselves again and again by convincing ourselves of the fact that it is only familiarity with the self-cherishing thought that causes it to arise habitually. Therefore, if we try to habituate our minds with the thought of cherishing others, then this thought will also arise in the same way. Shantideva says:

> It happens to us that, at one time, we can feel afraid even to hear the name of somebody we hate. Yet that same person often becomes so dear to us that we cannot bear to be without his or her presence, even for a short time. This comes through acquainting the mind with a positive attitude toward the person we previously hated.

The second obstacle that we often confront when meditating on bodhicitta is the habit of discriminating between ourself and others. Whenever we think of ourselves, deep down in our mind we project ourselves as being completely separate from those we project as being others. Under the influence of this thought we are only concerned with our own suffering and happiness, thinking of ourselves as being completely separate, just as the color blue is separate from yellow. We also fail to share sorrow and happiness with others by thinking that they are completely unrelated to us.

We should realize the fact that we and others are mutually dependent in terms of existence. Everything that we need in order to get rid of our suffering and achieve happiness, both at the temporary and ultimate level, entirely depends on our fellow beings. So we and others are not in fact two unrelated things, but are rather two parts of one whole. If we think about it, the only reason why we discriminate between ourselves and others is just because our thought projects ourself as being "me." It is the same for others: when they project themselves, they project themselves as being "me." Apart from this, we and others are in the same situation. Shantideva says:

> If we equalize ourselves with others, we will then be able to stabilize our practice of bodhicitta. We ourselves exist only because there are others. Just as the mountain where we dwell is projected as being "this side," the opposite side is projected as the "other side."

The third obstacle that often arises is the belief that our lives are limited to our own mind and body and that therefore we are by no means harmed by others' mental or physical sufferings. This selfish thought prevents us from developing the great sympathetic attitude of exchanging ourself with others and doing the practice of taking on their suffering and giving them our happiness (see page 130). It is this thought that stops us from sharing whatever sufferings others may face. Therefore, unless we can do something to get rid of, or at least subdue, this tricky thought, there is no hope for us to develop bodhicitta, which not only leads us to infinite happiness but also enables us to fulfill the happiness of countless beings.

We must realize that, since beginningless time, this cunning thought has dwelt in our hearts and has deceived us. Under the influence of this temptation we have been thinking only of ourselves; we have been seeking only our own happiness at the expense of others' happiness. As a result we have fallen countless times into the flames of the hot hells, experiencing immeasurable suffering. Now, however, we have fortunately gained the precious human rebirth, which provides us with incredible opportunities to become even enlightened within this very short lifetime. How foolish we would be if we still allowed ourselves to be the victim of this inner evil of the self-cherishing mind, while having so much wisdom power provided through this precious rebirth.

Although the minds and bodies of other beings do not belong to us in exactly the same way as our own belong to us, it is still foolish to believe that we should only think of our own happiness, be concerned only with our own suffering, and neglect others' suffering. It is this very thought that has brought us immeasurable and endless suffering since beginningless time.

Let us imagine how many rebirths we have taken in the past. We still have not achieved any stable and concrete happiness. If we ask ourselves why this is, the only answer is: because our minds are dominated by the self-cherishing thought.

Many beings before us, such as Lord Buddha Shakyamuni and Avalokiteshvara, the bodhisattva of compassion, have realized that the self-cherishing mind is the source of all suffering and cherishing others is the source of all happiness. As a result of this they gained the highest happiness and have been able to benefit countless beings.

Although the sufferings of others may not directly torture us as they do those who experience them, they still affect us in many ways. Also, it is much wiser to be concerned with others' suffering and happiness, not only from their point of view but from our point of view, too, because only this sympathetic thought enables us to get rid of the inner evil of cherishing ourself. The less selfish we are the happier we automatically become.

The thought that the suffering of others does not directly injure us and therefore does not concern us has no logical ground either. Lama Tsonghkapa says:

> Although the sufferings that we experience in the future do not directly affect us now, we are still concerned about them. Likewise, the happiness we may experience in the future does not directly give us pleasure at this very moment, yet we are still concerned about it. Thus, the thought that because others' suffering does not directly injure us and therefore does not concern us is neither a logical nor a moral way of thinking.

Similarly, Shantideva says:

> Although the foot suffers injury when a thorn pierces the skin, the hand will naturally act to relieve the pain by taking out the thorn, even though it does not directly experience pain itself. Why should we not be concerned and act to relieve others of suffering, although their suffering does not directly affect us?

We may think that since our foot experiences pain, the thorn does not directly hurt our hand. Yet both hand and foot belong to our body, so the hand naturally acts to release the pain that is experienced by the foot. Similarly, the sufferings or happiness that we will experience in the future do not affect us now, yet we who exist now and we who will exist in the future belong to the same continuum and we naturally act to prevent the suffering and achieve the happiness that we will experience in the future.

It is exactly the same with the suffering and happiness of others. We are all beings. Physically we may be separate, yet we have the same nature— wanting happiness and shunning suffering. So it is both logically and morally wrong to think that others' suffering does not directly injure us and their happiness does not directly give us pleasure and that therefore we should not be concerned about them.

Shantideva says:

All the happiness that exists in the world arises from the loving mind toward others. Similarly, all the suffering in the world arises from cherishing only ourselves. It is needless to say much about how cherishing others brings us happiness, while cherishing ourselves brings us suffering. Just look at the difference between Buddha, who has only been cherishing others, and us, who cherish only ourselves. Unless we get rid of this selfish thought, there is no way for us to achieve enlightenment, the highest happiness beyond cyclic existence, not to mention that we can hardly even be happy while we remain in cyclic existence.

Meditation on Exchanging Ourself with Others

All sentient beings have been my dear mother, father, brother, sister, and friend countless times and they have all been equally kind to me. All the happiness I have ever had in the past, have now, and will have in the future is due only to the kindness of my fellow beings. Yet I have been cherishing only myself and neglecting others since beginningless time. What could I achieve from this, my selfish attitude? Nothing but endless suffering. Under the influence of the inner demon of my self-cherishing thoughts, I have accumulated immeasurable negative karma. As a result I have been born in the hells again and again and have been tortured by unbearable sufferings.

Now, however, I have fortunately been able to obtain a precious human rebirth, which provides me with incredible abilities to judge what is right or wrong for myself and others. If I waste such abilities and allow myself to be influenced by my self-cherishing demon, then soon, when death comes, I will fall again into the immeasurable misery of the lower realms. Unless I subdue this evil demon, I will hardly be able to achieve happiness for myself, not to mention that I will be unable to fulfill the benefit of others.

There is no difference between myself and others in that we all equally shun even small discomforts and have an insatiable thirst for happiness. Therefore all sentient beings are equal to me from their point of view, because they shun suffering and desire happiness just as I do. From my point of view they are also equal to me, because all sentient beings have been equally kind to me. I shall equalize myself with all my mother beings.

Whatever suffering I experience arises from nowhere else but the evil thought of self-cherishing. Whatever happiness I have gained is due to the loving mind toward others. If I look at the difference between myself, who has cherished myself alone, and the Enlightened Ones, who cherish all others equally, it is very clear to see how my self-cherishing thoughts fool and deceive me and how the thoughts of cherishing others can awaken me from my ignorance and give me limitless happiness.

I shall remind myself of the incredible kindness that I receive from other sentient beings. They are not only kind to me when they are my parents, relatives, or friends, but they have always been kind to me, wherever I take rebirth, wherever I live, and wherever I go. All my happiness is entirely due to the kindness of others. Not only is the happiness that I achieve while in samsara due to their kindness, but achieving the highest happiness beyond samsara—enlightenment—also depends entirely upon the kindness of other sentient beings. I shall always show respect to them as I do to my spiritual guide, Buddha Shakyamuni.

I have now obtained the precious human rebirth, which provides me with incredible opportunities to achieve even enlightenment within this very short lifetime. But most of my mother beings are caught in the unbearable suffering of the lower realms. Their only hope is me. If I neglect them, how mindless I will be!

O my Guru Shakyamuni, please bestow your great compassion and wisdom upon me so that I can liberate all my mother beings from their endless suffering in samsara, by taking their suffering upon myself and giving them all my happiness.

Having contemplated in this way, we should recite the following verses composed by the great bodhisattva Atisha:

The Jewel Rosary of the Practice of Bodhicitta

I bow down to great compassion,
to all my spiritual masters,
and to my deities of devotion.

Having cast away all my doubts
about the value of spiritual practice,
I shall exert myself in the practice
of the Bodhisattva Path.

Having removed sleepiness, dullness, and laziness,
I shall always be joyful
when engaging in such powerful practices.

I shall guard the doors of my speech, body, and mind
against any negative action,
by constantly being alert and mindful in my behavior.
I shall examine my mind
over and over again, day and night.

I proclaim my faults, not seeking faults in others,
hide my own good qualities but praise those of others.
Not seeking material gain or veneration from others,
I will be able to abandon any desire for fame,
being content with whatever I have.
I shall not fail to repay whatever kindness
I receive from others
and shall meditate on love and compassion,
reminding myself always of bodhicitta,
the altruistic mind of enlightenment.

I abandon the ten non-virtuous actions
and consolidate my faith in spiritual practice.
Having abandoned pride over my qualities
and disdain toward others,
always humble,
I abandon wrong livelihood and follow right livelihood.

Having given up all meaningless activity,
I shall be endowed
with the inner jewel of Arya beings.
Having given up all meaningless activity,
I remain in solitude,
abandon senseless talk,
and discipline my speech.

Whenever I see my spiritual master
I pay respect from my heart,
and with equal respect
hold even ordinary sentient beings to be my great teachers,
as I hold great Arya beings to be.

Whenever I meet others
I regard older ones as my parents,
those of similar age or younger
as my brother, sister, or relative.

Having abandoned bad influence from others,
I shall follow spiritual friends,
be happy myself wherever I go,
without any ill-will toward others,
and not be discontented with my life.

I abandon attachment to any desirable things
and remain desireless,
for attachment in any form
can never lead to a happy rebirth.
Instead, it takes away the life-force
of liberation from suffering.

I shall exert myself in any virtuous activity
that can lead me to ultimate happiness,
accomplishing first whatever practices I have started.
Thus, I will be able to accomplish all my practices,

otherwise none of my tasks will be accomplished.
I take no interest in those activities
that can be harmful to others,
and cast away pride over my qualities
whenever it arises in my mind.
I must remind myself always
of the instructions of my spiritual teacher.

I shall be able to encourage myself
whenever I feel depressed,
whenever my mind is deluded by attachment to myself
and hatred toward others,
I shall be able to realize that both I and others
are equally void of inherent existence,
and view myself and others
as being illusory-like, a magic form.

Whenever I hear unpleasant words,
I view them as echoes.
Whenever my body is harmed by others,
I shall be able to view it as being
the result of my previous negative karma.

Abiding always in solitude,
like the corpse of a wild animal,
I shall keep myself away from the temptation
of meaningless activities,
and remain desireless,
reminding myself always of my deity of devotion.

Whenever laziness or laxity arise in my mind,
I shall be able to remove them immediately
and always remember the essence of moral behavior.

Whenever I meet others,
Having removed angry behavior,

I shall be able to speak sincerely and frankly,
with a smiling face.

Whenever I meet others,
I shall not be jealous of them,
but be generous to them.
I abandon any dispute with others
and concern myself with their welfare and comfort.

I shall not be fickle in any relationships with others,
but remain firm.
I give up any form of humiliating others
and always respect them.

Whenever I give advice to others,
I shall do so with sincerity and sympathy.
I abandon any disrespect for other forms of spiritual practice
and appreciate whatever religions
others are interested in.
I shall be able to remain with the practice of the ten virtues, day
    and night.
I dedicate whatever virtues I have done in the past,
do now, and will do in the future,
to the benefit of other sentient beings.

Through performing the Seven Limb Prayer
I pray for the happiness of all other beings.

Thus I will be able to accomplish
the merit of wisdom and skillful means,
and will be able to eliminate all delusions,
for in this way,
I shall be able to attain enlightenment
for the sake of all sentient beings.
Thus I will be able to achieve great meaning
from finding this precious human rebirth.

There are seven gems that adorn the minds of bodhisattvas:
the gem of faith,
the gem of instruction,
the gem of contemplation,
the gem of wisdom,
the gem of ethics,
the gem of modesty,
and the gem of generosity.

These seven gems have limitless virtuous qualities.
When I practice these inner gems within myself,
I should not reveal any to those
who are not yet mature to practice these excellent qualities.

I shall be heedful of my speech
in the presence of others,
and be heedful of my thoughts
in isolation from others.

4. Meditation on Giving Our Own Happiness to Others and Taking Their Suffering Upon Ourself

After reciting the above verses, we should do the following visualization known as giving and taking (Tibetan *tong len*):

Light radiates from the crown, throat, and heart chakras of the buddhas and bodhisattvas in the merit field, enters our heart and purifies our self-cherishing mind.

Then the sufferings of all other beings appear in the form of black smoke. As we breathe in, we inhale this black smoke into our heart and firmly think that we have taken all their sufferings upon ourself.

Then, while breathing out, we send all our happiness visualized in the form of white light, to others. Firmly think that we have given them all our happiness.

At this point we should recite the following verse several times, reflecting on its meaning:

Bless me, my Guru Shakyamuni,
so that I can quickly take upon myself
all the sufferings of other sentient beings
and lead them to great happiness,
by giving them all my happiness, good deeds,
and whatever else I have.

PART FIVE

The Six Perfections

Asanga

12. Encouraging Ourselves to Practice the Bodhisattva Path

When true bodhicitta—the altruistic mind of enlightenment—arises within us we will naturally seek the best possible method for liberating other fellow beings from their suffering. Here Lord Buddha said in the sutra *Request by the Bodhisattva Named Great Ocean of Wisdom*:

> Suppose you have an only child who is very dear to you. If you were to see your beloved one drowning in a great ocean full of ruthless, fierce monsters, you would immediately do everything possible to rescue him or her—you could not bear to leave your child under such terrible conditions.
>
> In the same way, when bodhisattvas see all mother sentient beings drowning in the ageless and bottomless ocean of suffering within cyclic existence, being tortured again and again by rebirth, sickness, old age, and death, their minds are boundlessly moved by unceasing compassion. They devote themselves to seeking every possible way to rescue their mother beings as soon as possible.

These words of Buddha show how bodhisattvas dedicate themselves to liberating other sentient beings. If we truly see how all other beings have been our beloved mother and how they have endlessly been caught in the ageless suffering of cyclic existence, a great sympathy, wishing them to be free from suffering, will arise in us. Generating such sympathy alone has great value, as Lord Buddha often stated in many Mahayana sutras:

Even if we generate bodhicitta for one moment, the amount of merit that we will gain is measureless.

Nevertheless, it is not sufficient to have such a good heart alone if we are truly concerned about liberating other fellow beings from their suffering. Therefore we need to inspire ourselves to actually do something to rescue our mother beings from the suffering of cyclic existence. Here, to quote Nagarjuna:

> Only an enlightened being is fully equipped with all the qualities that can fulfill the needs of all sentient beings; therefore those who wish to help all living beings to be freed from cyclic existence should seek to attain enlightenment.

Hence our highest aim should be to attain the state of enlightenment.

We have the potential to attain enlightenment. What is the method? On the one hand, getting rid of our own delusions, and on the other, developing sincere sympathy toward others and engaging in the activities of benefiting them. The path to enlightenment therefore has two aspects: (1) purifying our own mind of delusions and (2) developing the skillful means for benefiting others.

Buddha taught this path on the basis of the six perfections:

1   generosity
2   morality
3   patience
4   enthusiastic perseverance
5   single-pointed mind
6   wisdom

In the sutra called *Request by Ösung* Buddha says:

> Just as kings are able to fulfill their royal affairs only when they are supported by many expert ministers, likewise wisdom can lead to enlightenment only when complemented with the full practice of other skillful means such as the practice of generosity, morality, and

so on. Therefore bodhisattvas should practice the completion of all aspects of the six perfections.

And in the sutra called *The Teachings of Gaya Guri* he adds:

The path to enlightenment is twofold: wisdom and skillful means. The practice of the first four perfections is the practice of skillful means. The last two perfections reveal the practice of wisdom.

To gain ultimate wisdom we need the power of merit or positive energy. The highest merit we can gain is from benefiting others, therefore Buddha also taught the practice of the four skillful means, which provides us with excellent methods for benefiting others:

1 The skill of being able to fulfill the material needs of others.
2 The skill of being able to give whatever Dharma instructions others require.
3 The skill of being able to practice Dharma ourselves.
4 The skill of being able to practice whatever instructions we give others.

The practices of the six perfections and four skillful means contain all the methods and skills required for eliminating our own delusions and fulfilling the needs of others as well. Therefore it is necessary to practice all aspects of the six perfections and four skillful means if we truly wish to attain the enlightened state.

These practices of the bodhisattva not only enable us to fulfill the needs of our fellow beings but also lead us from happy to happier states. The practice of wisdom helps us to subdue our own deluded mind so that we can maintain pure speech and physical activity. This in turn leads us continuously to happy rebirths in the higher realms. Moreover, as most of our suffering and problems arise from our own unsubdued mind, if we develop wisdom we are easily able to control our own delusions and thus retain a very joyful and happy frame of mind, regardless of external difficulties that we may face in our lives.

13. Introducing the Six Perfections

The Meaning of Perfection

The practices of the six perfections are called *paramita* in Sanskrit, meaning "reaching beyond limitation," because they lead us to the attainment of the fully developed wisdom that has reached beyond limitation. Here the Indian Master Shantipa said in his commentary on Maitreya's *Ornament for Clear Realization*:

> True perfection is the fully developed state of wisdom. Because the wisdom that realizes the ultimate truth leads us to this fully developed state of wisdom, beyond any limitation, it is named "perfection." The practices of generosity, morality, patience, enthusiastic perseverance, and single-pointed mind help us to cultivate this wisdom so that we can travel toward the perfection of wisdom. Thus they are also named "perfection."

Therefore, to achieve the perfection of wisdom, which is the highest aim of the bodhisattva, we need to practice all the other perfections fully.

The main reason why bodhisattvas seek the perfection of wisdom is that their goal is to release all other sentient beings from their suffering. Only the perfection of wisdom has the full power to do so. Thus if we truly wish to attain the perfection of wisdom in order to benefit other sentient beings, it is not sufficient for us to develop wisdom alone; we also need to engage in extensive skillful activities to benefit other fellow beings. It is clear to see how the practice of each of the six perfections helps us to fulfill this goal of developing our own wisdom and of benefiting others if we look at the significance of the practices of these six perfections. Here, Maitreya stated in his *Ornament to the Mahayana Sutras*:

> The first perfection is called generosity because it releases others from poverty. The second perfection is named morality because it releases us from feelings of remorse. Since the third perfection enables us to overcome difficulties, it is called patience. Through the fourth perfection, enthusiastic perseverance, we make progress in our practice. The fifth enables us to concentrate single-pointedly on any object, therefore it is called single-pointed mind. And the sixth perfection is called wisdom, or ultimate knowledge, because it is through this that we realize the ultimate truth.

No matter how much effort we make to develop wisdom, we will not be able to achieve the perfection of wisdom unless we engage in the practices of other skillful means, such as generosity and so forth, because perfect wisdom is the wisdom that is fully equipped with all the other virtuous qualities that are necessary to fulfill the needs of other beings.

The Order of Practicing the Six Perfections

The Buddha taught the practice of generosity first, then morality, patience, enthusiastic perseverance, single-pointed mind, and wisdom, in that order. Buddha leads us to the easier practices first, then, once we are advanced, to the higher practices. It is easier to practice generosity than to practice morality; and it is easier to practice morality than to practice patience, and so on. Therefore Buddha encouraged us to practice generosity first, then morality and so forth.

Furthermore, the practices of the former perfections help us to form the basis for the latter ones. For example, the practice of generosity provides us with a sound basis for developing morality. The reason for this is that the main obstacle to the development of pure morality is attachment to our own possessions. The most powerful antidote to this attachment is generosity.

Likewise, the practice of morality forms the foundation to develop patience because through the practice of morality we are able to control our own delusions, so that we can retain constant peace and tranquility, even when facing difficulties in our lives.

Patience is the strength of mind that enables us to face any difficulties without losing our inner tranquility and calmness. Without the strength of patience we will not be able to maintain enthusiasm in our practice. Thus, the practice of patience helps us to develop enthusiastic perseverance.

Single-pointed mind is the fully trained state of mind and is not easy to achieve. To develop such a state we need unceasing enthusiasm, hence developing enthusiastic perseverance is the real foundation for developing a single-pointed mind.

Wisdom is the clear state of mind that can uninterruptedly penetrate into the subtle nature of the object of meditation. Such a clear state of wisdom arises only when our mind is calm and well-concentrated. Thus, single-pointed mind provides us with the sound foundation for cultivating wisdom.

From this we can see how important it is for us to practice the six perfections in a sequential way.

When we generate true compassion and a loving mind equally toward all beings, our main concern will be to release others from their suffering and lead them to happiness. The practice of the six perfections will fulfill this goal.

We may do many things for others but we cannot be of pure service to others unless we subdue our own deluded mind. The perfect method for disciplining and eventually subduing our own deluded mind is contained in the practices of the last two perfections—single-pointed mind and wisdom. Through developing these we will achieve great calmness and tranquility. However, bodhisattvas do not seek these just to release themselves from suffering; they seek these inner qualities in order to be able to benefit other beings effectively and purely.

The practices of generosity, morality, patience, and enthusiastic perseverance enable us to fulfill the goal of benefiting our fellow beings. If we are able to be sincerely generous we can release others from their poverty and fear and eventually lead them completely beyond the suffering of cyclic existence.

Even though we may have the good intention to help other beings we will not be able to benefit them purely unless we give up our own harmful thoughts and actions. The practice of morality is to refrain from engaging in harmful thoughts and actions. The most important thing that we need in order to accomplish our goal of benefiting others is unceasing determination. This power can be achieved only when and if we develop patience and enthusiastic perseverance.

The Way of Practicing the Six Perfections

In *The Compendium of Mahayana Teachings* the great Indian scholar, Asanga, explained how bodhisattvas practice the six perfections on the basis of what he called the six nobilities. These reflect the motivation, stages, the actual method, and the result of practicing the six perfections.

The first nobility, *the nobility of the base*, refers to generating a pure motivation to practice the six perfections. When we generate sincere compassion and love equally toward all mother beings, then it becomes natural for us to be concerned about their welfare. The perfect method with which we can help mother beings to be free from suffering and lead them to everlasting happiness is the practice of the six perfections. Therefore, if we sincerely and truly want to benefit our mother beings, we should practice these perfections in our daily life with a pure motivation.

The second nobility, *the nobility of the object*, states the importance of taking pure and extensive instructions from Buddha on the practices of the six perfections. Without full knowledge of what we are going to practice, we will not be able to accomplish our goal, even though we may have a good motivation. The great Tsonghkapa always emphasized that seeking knowledge is as important as practicing what we have learned. Since we seek the knowledge of the six perfections not only for our own gain, but to be able to benefit mother beings purely, our study itself becomes a very important practice.

Although we may have generated a good motivation at the beginning, it can happen that in the course of study and practice we forget our original motivation and become egocentric. Therefore, it is very important to maintain and increase our motivation to benefit others constantly. This is what is emphasized in the third nobility, *the nobility of the goal*.

The fourth nobility, *the nobility of dedication*, indicates the practice of pure dedication. Whenever we engage in the practice of the six perfections, at the end we should dedicate whatever merit we have gained from it, purely, to benefit mother beings. In a bodhisattva's practice dedicating the merits is part of the practice of exchanging self with others. We not only benefit others through our practice of the six perfections, but also give them whatever results we will gain from our practice. Therefore, this is a very powerful practice to cut through our own self-cherishing attitude.

To practice the six perfections effectively, we require a great deal of skill because we can quite often face many difficulties. For example, we can lose patience or become disheartened; also our practice can become deluded by egocentric attitudes. It is important to check again and again whether our practice is influenced by ego, pride, or selfish gain. The main method to cut egocentric attitudes is the realization of emptiness. Therefore, when bodhisattvas engage in these practices, they do so in conjunction with wisdom, realizing that both the practitioner and the practice are void of self-existence. This is the fifth nobility, *the nobility of skill*. With wisdom we are enabled to encourage ourselves whenever we face any difficulties in our practice. Thus, we develop great skills through our experience in overcoming difficulties.

Skill also means to practice according to our ability. In the practice of giving, for example, we mentally practice giving our body in meditation. Once we reach a high level on the Bodhisattva Path we are allowed to give our body away—to a hungry animal, for example.

The sixth nobility, *the nobility of purity*, refers to the result of practicing the six perfections. The ultimate result that we will gain is enlightenment, the final goal of bodhisattvas. Only bodhisattvas, those who are deeply concerned about the suffering of other sentient beings, are keen to seek the attainment of enlightenment. If we are only interested in liberating ourself from suffering, it is not necessary to dedicate ourself to the extensive practice and difficulties of the Bodhisattva Path; we can gain self-liberation through a much simpler and easier path. However, if we have strong sympathy toward other sentient beings who equally suffer, then it is important to seek the best possible way to benefit them. This can only be done when we have achieved the enlightened state.

Explanation of the First Four Perfections

Let us remind ourselves of how important it is to generate a good heart toward others and find ways of actually helping them. Not only do we wish to relieve mother sentient beings from their temporary sufferings, but we also wish them to be free from the root of all suffering, their delusions.

Only the wisdom that realizes the ultimate truth has the power to eliminate our delusions from their root. To be able to lead others, we must first realize this truth within ourselves. Shantideva says:

> Buddha taught all other practices of skillful means—generosity and so on—for the sake of cultivating the wisdom that realizes the ultimate truth.

So, for the sake of developing this wisdom as well as to benefit others directly, let us look at how to practice these perfections in our daily life.

1. The Perfection of Generosity

Practicing generosity means dedicating ourselves to helping or benefiting those who are in need. This practice transforms all our positive energies into the actual way of benefiting others. Buddha taught three different ways of practicing generosity: offering material help to those who suffer from a lack of material necessities; giving protection to those in fear; giving sincere and pure instruction.

Buddha mentioned various beings who are worthy of being given material help. They are the Three Jewels: Buddha, Dharma, and Sangha; those who purely dedicate their lives to spiritual practice; those who have been kind to us; those who are helpless; those who are desperately in need of help; those who suffer from poverty; the sick; and the old. Although in general any beings who are in need are objects of the practice of generosity, it is more worthwhile if we give our material help to these.

There are many good opportunities to practice generosity in our everyday life. For instance, when we hear of someone facing a great tragedy, or overcome by fear when trapped in a fire, or drowning, or when we hear that sick or old people are being neglected, this gives us a good opportu-

nity to practice the perfection of generosity. It is the true practice of bodhisattvas that whenever such an opportunity comes they joyfully go to help
in whichever way they can. In the West many people are concerned about
protecting animals from cruelty and also protecting children from being
neglected. We should try to feel that it is our personal responsibility and
sincerely help in any way we can.

Giving genuine and pure instruction to others does not only refer to giving philosophical teachings; giving any helpful advice in a sincere way is
also the practice of generosity. Therefore, it is very important for us to
advise people and guide them, enabling them to sort out their problems in
a positive way. It is helpful to regard those who are older than us as our parents, those of similar age as our brothers or sisters, and younger ones as our
sons or daughters.

The benefits to be gained from the perfection of generosity are measureless. Not only does it release others from suffering and problems, but
it will also bring us great wealth in future lifetimes. This does not mean that
bodhisattvas practice generosity just because they desire wealth, but they
can be of greater benefit if they have plenty to give.

When we practice generosity there are four very important factors that
we should bear in mind: pure motivation, respectful behavior, great skill,
and correct dedication.

There are three impure motivations to be abandoned. The first is giving material help to others but with bad intent. For instance, people sometimes give a lot of money with the intention of harming those they hate.
This is not the pure practice of generosity because its intention is wrong.

The second impure motivation is lack of respect. When we give material help to others, our intention might not be to harm them but genuinely
to help. Yet sometimes we forget to show respect to those who ask for help.
We may look down on them or humiliate them, or we may be tempted to
think how great we are and feel proud. If we want to practice generosity
purely, then this kind of attitude must be abandoned. Bodhisattvas always
regard those who come to beg for any material help from them as their
great spiritual master and show enormous respect.

The third wrong motivation is expectation. If we sincerely want to
practice the perfection of generosity, then it is very important for us to try
not to have any expectations. The kind of attitude we should generate is

that we should regard those we are helping as our great spiritual master, regardless of whether they are highly realized persons or deluded ones, poor or rich. We should show them great respect and must make sure that our motivation is really to benefit them and not expect any kind of reward.

Another important thing to be aware of is the purpose of giving help. What this means is that we should thoroughly check on whether the help we give is going to harm others. Sometimes our motivation may be correct from our side and we feel no miserliness toward our possessions, but unskillful giving of help can sometimes harm others.

There are many incorrect ways of behaving that we should give up. Sometimes, out of habit, we complain when needy people come to us for material help. We may even use unpleasant words or behave impolitely. We should give up any incorrect behavior, such as purposely showing off our kindness by telling others how we have helped; handing over things in a disrespectful way; using harsh words; humiliating others by saying, "How poor you are! How greedy you are!" and so on.

Kadampa lamas always try to train themselves in how to behave toward others before they engage in any activity of giving. Bodhisattvas always try to be respectful and polite. Even though we may give a lot of material help to others, if our motivation and way of giving is not correct, this spoils our practice. Tsonghkapa says:

No one is forcing us to practice Dharma. If we want to practice, it is better to do so in a pure way. Then it becomes fruitful.

Dharma practice has so much to do with motivation and behavior, our way of conducting ourselves. We as beginners, however, still have a lot of selfish desire toward our possessions, so we cannot expect ourselves to be able to give them all away, as great bodhisattvas can do. Here Lord Buddha said in the sutra called *Request by the Bodhisattva Pung Zang*:

If somebody turns up at your door and begs, and you cannot fulfill that person's wish because of your own selfish desire for your possessions, then first try to remind yourself of the impermanent nature of your wealth and life and try to fulfill the beggar's wish. If you are still unable to be generous, you should politely ask for forgiveness and then pray to be able to practice generosity soon.

In the practice of generosity it is not a case of giving everything straight away, regardless of our genuine ability, but it is a matter of sincerely giving as much as we can.

There is great skill involved in the practice of giving. This means to be fully aware of whether our charity is going to be harmful or beneficial. There are many unskillful charitable actions, for instance, killing small animals such as birds or deer to feed bigger ones, such as tigers; or killing fish to feed the birds; or giving money for weapons. Similarly, it would be unskillful generosity to give alcohol or cigarettes.

When we have practiced giving we should remember to dedicate. Not only do bodhisattvas not expect anything in return when they practice generosity, but they also dedicate whatever merit they gain to the happiness of others.

2. The Perfection of Morality

Morality means to refrain from any negative or unwholesome mental, verbal, and physical actions. There are ten non-virtues: four of speech—telling lies, gossiping, using harsh words, slander; three of body—killing, stealing, sexual misconduct; three of mind—craving, the thought to harm, wrong views. When we refrain from these our mind naturally becomes clear and calm. On the basis of such a mind we can develop another aspect of morality: cultivating positive states of mind such as bodhicitta and love. As we develop our moral conduct with sincerity and love, we should also lead others to the practice of morality.

The practice of morality is very important. In order to gain any higher realizations, what we first need is a still and stable mind. Obviously there is no way to gain this as long as we are under the influence of delusions such as anger, insatiable desire, pride, and so on. Buddha therefore taught the practice of morality, which is the perfect method for turning the mind away from the influence of delusions. Most of the gross delusions arise from engaging in negative actions, for example, drinking too much alcohol.

The practice of morality therefore guards us from any harmful influences that might cause delusions to arise. Our mind automatically becomes free from gross disturbances. This is why Buddha says that morality is the foundation of single-pointed mind.

For bodhisattvas the practice of morality has far more purpose than just to gain peace for themselves. For example, Buddha says:

> Even though we give help to others, if we do not give up harming them, our generosity will not be pure.

One of the fundamental practices of bodhisattvas is to respect all living beings equally, just as they respect Buddha. Therefore, the practice of morality is always to be mindful not to generate any thought of harming others, not to utter any harmful or harsh words and not to engage in any harmful or impolite actions.

The vows that bodhisattvas take deal with this kind of morality or discipline. Therefore, we must first be familiar with them and know how to maintain them with mindfulness and great awareness. There are four things to avoid, otherwise known as doors of transgression.

The first is not knowing what we should abandon and what we should take up. If we do not know the vows and how to maintain them, we might unknowingly engage in unwholesome actions.

The second is being careless about our speech, thoughts, and actions. Although we may know what unwholesome actions are and how to guard ourselves from them, if we remain heedless in our daily life, we will not be able to maintain pure morality. This is the case for many of us. We may know what the ten non-virtues are, for example, but in our day-to-day lives we often ignore them. Because of this, we fail to guard our speech, body, and mind from the ten non-virtuous actions. Therefore, it is very important for us to be mindful by keeping a close check on our thoughts, speech, and physical actions.

Mindfulness does not only mean to reflect on virtuous and non-virtuous actions in meditation sessions. It is the range of our awareness or heedfulness throughout our lives, day and night. Here Atisha says:

Most of us think that the practice of Dharma is to recite some commitment and visualize a deity or chant, but real Dharma practice is the integration of virtuous activities into our lives. If we are aware of this, we might gain more realizations in our daily lives than during our sitting meditations.

Sometimes we do not pay much attention to our moral practice because we do not have much respect for it. This is the third door of transgression. Therefore, we need to remind ourselves of the importance of keeping moral conduct purely. We can hardly achieve any realizations without having pure morality as the basis.

We know how difficult it is to keep our mind calm and peaceful. We think it is only meditation that makes our mind calm and peaceful, so we do not care very much about our daily moral conduct. No matter how much we try to meditate, it is very difficult to gain stability and stillness of mind as long as we neglect to keep our daily moral practice purely. So it is moral practice that initially brings peace and calmness to our mind, not meditation or sitting cross-legged and visualizing things. Many Kadampa lamas say:

If we keep moral practice purely, day and night, our mind automatically becomes calm and clear.

The fourth door of transgression is increasing our delusions. What is important here is that we should check again and again whether any delusion is arising within our mind. If we find one arising, we should not fail to contemplate on the antidote. For instance, when we find our desire increasing, we should meditate on the impermanent nature of life; when anger increases, try to meditate on love and compassion. See pages 176–78 for more details of these.

The practice of morality is important for us if we sincerely intend to practice the Bodhisattva Path. It is a vast and profound practice because it provides us with a firm ground for accomplishing our goal of benefiting other sentient beings. By practicing morality we abandon harming any living being in any way whatsoever. On the basis of this we practice the perfection of giving in order to benefit others in a practical way. This is the perfect way through which past and present buddhas have attained the enlightened state, thereby ceaselessly benefiting countless beings.

3. The Perfection of Patience

Practicing patience does not mean being passive or withdrawing from difficult situations or hardships. Rather it is an inner strength, which enables us to face problems in a positive way. It enables us to keep sight of our goal and not lose courage. Patience is a most excellent quality; it is the firmness of our inner understanding. If we come to understand the deeper cause of our problems rather than blame the temporary conditions created by others, we will be able to be firm and not become agitated when facing difficulties. We will not let ourselves be victimized by temporary disturbance, but will respond to the problem with a positive solution.

Buddhism explains three different types of patience: the patience of forgiveness; the patience of being able to accept suffering; and the patience of being able to engage in virtuous practice.

The essence of the patience of forgiveness is to be firm and positive whenever others criticize or cause us trouble. Normally our reaction is to become angry and return the harm because we lack patience. Impatience not only leads to the endless trouble of quarrels but makes us unhappy, too. Tsonghkapa said that we cannot really rest or be happy as long as we remain impatient, and impatience brings endless anxiety and worry. Therefore, if we truly wish to remain in peace and happiness, we should first consolidate our practice of developing patience. Similarly, Shantideva said that we cannot even have a short, restful sleep with an impatient attitude, not to mention how much trouble it brings us.

As long as we remain within cyclic existence, we can hardly expect not to meet with trouble or come across people we dislike or someone who hates us. Samsaric life itself is in the nature of suffering. Usually, our attitude toward those we dislike or those who cause us trouble is quite negative and we blame everything on them. This attitude is what makes us feel angry or resentful toward others. If we want to get rid of anger, then we should first give up this negative attitude toward our so-called enemy.

Here Shantideva said that we should initially check the situation of those who cause the trouble, to see whether they have any control over themselves at that moment. When we investigate this, we will clearly see that the person who hurts or beats us or just causes trouble is in the same situation as ourself. Sometimes, out of jealousy, an unhappy mood, or out of desire for position or fame, we ourselves also say negative things to others. We gossip, slander, and play little games to harm others indirectly. Those who harm us are in the same situation. We want happiness and do not want suffering. We are afraid of suffering; so are those who harm us. Therefore, we can see that there is no difference between ourself and our so-called enemy.

When we use harsh words or cause someone trouble or harm, we can see that we ourselves are totally subject to our deluded mind. We have no control when negative thoughts dominate our mind and we deliberately harm others. When others harm us, they also have no control over their mind. Nobody wants suffering or problems, so we can be sure that neither we nor our so-called enemies want trouble. Yet under the obsession of our inner demon, our delusions, we harm each other. Therefore, we should look at those who trouble us as persons who are uncontrollably obsessed by their delusions, like someone completely obsessed by an evil spirit.

When we come to realize this, we are able to accept whatever trouble others cause us. To accept trouble does not mean to be cowardly. Patience is the bravest attitude, because with patience we can remain without fear even in the most difficult situation. Acceptance of suffering means to understand the situation of others with an open mind. With this understanding we can easily forgive them.

The second type of patience is to endure whatever suffering and problems we encounter. This is a very important practice. Whenever we face any suffering or problems, if we view them negatively, then this brings even more mental unhappiness in addition to the problems themselves. Therefore, the best way to endure or accept the problems is to view them in a positive way, as explained in the practice of thought transformation (Tibetan *lo jong*). In this practice it says that suffering or problems have many great qualities, if we are only aware of them. It helps us learn many useful lessons to improve our inner strength. All great beings gained their inner strength from facing difficulties. It also helps to reduce our pride, as well as understanding the situation of others. Therefore, if we look at our problems in a positive way, we begin to realize that we can gain many advantages from experiencing them.

The third type of patience refers to the ability to engage in virtuous practice, particularly the ability to penetrate deeper into the object of meditation.

4. The Perfection of Enthusiastic Perseverance

Enthusiastic perseverance is essential in the practice of any virtue, particularly when we practice the Bodhisattva Path. Enthusiastic perseverance means having a very joyful attitude toward virtuous practice. This arises from seeing the great value in practicing a virtuous path, therefore it is important that we remind ourselves again and again of the great benefit we can gain from practicing the Bodhisattva Path. When we see the benefit deeply and clearly, we easily feel joyful at developing virtuous practice. This is the first type of enthusiastic perseverance.

To maintain great determination, regardless of any difficulty we may face in the course of our practice, is very important; this is the second type of enthusiastic perseverance, so-called great determination. Whenever we face any difficulty in the course of our practice, we should encourage ourselves not to lose our strength, by reminding ourselves of the great many benefits that we can gain from the practice of the Bodhisattva Path.

The third practice of enthusiastic perseverance is developing encouragement. We should often remind ourselves that we have Buddha potential and remember how fortunate we are to have perfect circumstances to practice even the highest teachings.

The perfections of single-pointed mind and wisdom are explained in chapters 15, 16, 17, and 18.

Four Aspects of Each of the Six Perfections

In his *Ornament to Mahayana Sutras* Maitreya explained the nature of each of the six perfections. They are characterized by four aspects: purity, wisdom, the function of fulfilling the benefit of others, and leading others to the completion of the six perfections, or the Dharmakaya state.

The Four Aspects of Generosity

The practice of generosity is the selfless state of mind that enables us to give whatever we have to help others. When bodhisattvas practice this perfection, they sincerely give whatever others request with great joy and without any miserliness. This is the aspect of purity. Being aware of emptiness (ultimate truth), bodhisattvas always see that the giver, that which is given, and the persons to whom they are giving, are all empty of inherent existence. This is the aspect of wisdom. To fulfill the desire of others, bodhisattvas always offer things in a respectful manner. Thus they joyfully please others and benefit them. Whenever bodhisattvas practice generosity, they not only satisfy the desires of those who make requests, but they also gradually lead them to the path of liberation and eventually to the path of enlightenment.

The Four Aspects of Morality

The practice of morality is the state of great awareness, whereby we can guard ourselves against committing any non-virtuous actions of mind, speech, and body. The aspect of purity is turning our mind, body, and speech away from the influence of non-virtuous activities. Whenever bodhisattvas practice morality, they are always aware that the practice itself and the practitioner are equally empty of self-existence. This is the aspect of wisdom. By practicing morality, bodhisattvas prevent others from getting harmed and thus benefit them. They not only give up harming others, but also lead them on the path to liberation and eventually to enlightenment through their practice of morality.

The Four Aspects of Patience

Patience is the mental strength that enables us to overcome any harm from others or any difficulties that we confront. We develop it by understanding positive ways of looking at difficult situations. The practice of patience gives rise to great inner strength, enabling us to let go of any anger or ill-will that may arise when we face difficult situations. This is the aspect of purity. When bodhisattvas practice patience, they always do so in conjunction with wisdom, realizing that those who cause harm, the action of harming, and those to whom harm is done are all equally empty of self-existence. Through the practice of patience, bodhisattvas are able to benefit even those who bear them ill-will. Not only do bodhisattvas give up the wish to retaliate when they are harmed, but through the practice of patience, they also joyfully lead others to enlightenment.

The Four Aspects of Enthusiastic Perseverance

Enthusiastic perseverance is the feeling of joyfulness at doing virtuous actions. This perfection gives us unceasing energy, so that we are able to accomplish all our practices. As we feel very enthusiastic toward our practice, there is no room for any kind of laziness to delude our minds. This perfection is the most important one for developing realizations, for with it there is no feeling of hardship of any kind, and we can accomplish the practice of any higher path that we follow. This is the aspect of purity. As with the first three perfections, this one is also said to be practiced in conjunction with wisdom, realizing that those who practice this perfection and the actual practice of it are both equally empty of inherent existence. The practice of enthusiastic perseverance constantly gives us tremendous energy to take on any task for the benefit of others. Thus, we are able to fulfill whatever other beings desire. The last aspect is that bodhisattvas never give up their task of benefiting others until they have led them to the enlightened state.

The Four Aspects of Single-Pointed Mind

Single-pointed mind, or samatha, is the calm and fully trained state of the meditative mind. It is completely free from mental dullness and disturbance. This is the aspect of purity. When bodhisattvas practice samatha, they always practice it in conjunction with wisdom, realizing that the meditator and the object of meditation are both equally empty of self-existence. Through samatha bodhisattvas gain great miraculous powers whereby they can benefit many sentient beings. Bodhisattvas aspire to attain the highest state of single-pointed mind, not just to have peace away from samsaric disturbance, but to be able to help others gain freedom from the suffering of cyclic existence. Thus, they use whatever mental powers they develop for the sole purpose of leading sentient beings to the enlightened state.

The Four Aspects of Wisdom

Wisdom is the realization that whatever is impermanent by nature is impermanent; whatever is suffering by nature is suffering; whatever is impure by nature is impure; and whatever is lacking in inherent existence by nature is empty of inherent existence. Wisdom is the direct antidote to ignorance, which lies at the root of all delusion. This is the aspect of purity.

Whenever bodhisattvas practice wisdom, they always practice it in conjunction with skillful means. Wisdom enables bodhisattvas to see clearly how they can fulfill the needs of other sentient beings. Thus, through wisdom, bodhisattvas never fail to fulfill the needs of others. The ultimate goal of the bodhisattva is to lead others to the enlightened state. The only way to lead them is by helping them to cultivate wisdom within themselves. Thus, bodhisattvas develop wisdom, not for the sake of liberating themselves from suffering, but to lead others to enlightenment.

Tara

14. Meditations on the First Four Perfections

First we should visualize the merit field, perform the Seven Limb Prayer, and offer the mandala as described in the preliminary practices, pages 35–56. Having done this, contemplate in the following manner:

1. Meditation on the Perfection of Generosity

At this time I have obtained the precious human rebirth through which I can achieve even enlightenment within this very short lifetime. To have such an incredible opportunity is extremely rare, therefore it is time for me to seek something meaningful, not only to gain a happy rebirth for myself, but also to repay the kindness I have received from all my fellow beings.

If I sincerely and deeply discern, every single happiness I have achieved from beginningless time, have now, and will have in the future is due to the kindness of these fellow beings. Therefore, at this precious time I should not waste the great potential I have achieved and should try to attain a more meaningful goal, not only for my own happiness but also for the benefit of all my mother beings.

Henceforth, I shall devote myself wholeheartedly to the great bodhisattvas such as the great compassionate Avalokiteshvara, the great wise Manjushri, and the great loving Maitreya, who purely and fully dedicated their lives to the benefit of all beings. I shall follow sincerely the spiritual path they have traveled in order to benefit countless beings. Not only did they give their material prosperity purely to benefit others, they even sacrificed their own most precious lives for them. As a result of their incredible practice of selfless generosity, they have been able to benefit countless beings, leading them completely to true liberation from suffering, not to mention the immeasurable happiness they have achieved for themselves.

If I look at my situation, since beginningless time I have been thinking only of my own selfish interest. What have I gained from all this selfishness? Nothing but endless suffering. Let me remind myself of how many lifetimes I have wasted in this selfish attitude... However, at this time, I feel I am most fortunate to have met the stainless teachings of Lord Buddha and through these I know which is the right path to follow and which is not. From now on in my everyday life I shall practice the great jewel of the bodhisattvas—the perfection of generosity.

I owe whatever happiness and prosperity I have now to the kindness of all my fellow beings. It is through their kindness that I have achieved it all. Yet whatever prosperity and happiness I have is subject to impermanence. Unless I use it meaningfully, soon, when death comes, I will have no choice but to leave everything behind without having achieved any benefit from it. Moreover, if I do not realize the truth of impermanence, then the good fortune and wealth I have now will cause my attachment and desire to increase. As a result of that, when I depart from this life, leaving everything behind, I will fall back into the immeasurable suffering of rebirth in the lower realms. Therefore, I shall use whatever prosperity I have to achieve a meaningful goal.

Whenever I see or hear of the misery and impoverishment of other beings, I shall be able to recognize them as being the same as myself, who shuns even the slightest suffering and thirsts after happiness, and shall benefit them as much as I can.

2. Meditation on the Perfection of Morality

Since beginningless time my mind has been influenced by the evil of delusions. I have been attached to my own happiness alone and have disregarded others. As a result of this I have gone through unimaginable suffering. Buddha says that the source of happiness, for ourselves and for those around us, is the practice of morality: restraining ourselves completely from engaging in harmful actions, physically, verbally, and mentally. Moreover, I am trying to follow the path of the bodhisattvas. I will not be able to benefit others sincerely unless I am first able to give up causing any harm to any being.

Through the practice of morality all buddhas and bodhisattvas not only have measureless happiness for themselves, but are enabled to lead countless beings beyond all the sufferings of cyclic existence. Hence, if I am truly honest with myself and am sincerely concerned with benefiting all my mother beings, there is no greater practice than to follow the great path of the bodhisattvas—the perfection of morality.

Buddha called the perfection of morality the "jewel of the bodhisattvas." This practice is truly a jewel because it will not only bring limitless happiness to those who practice it, but will also fulfill the needs of countless beings.

The great bodhisattvas dedicated their lives to the benefit of countless beings; I shall follow their example. Whenever I see or hear about others in misery or suffering from hunger or thirst, I shall be able to recognize them as my mother and help to release them from their misery. Whenever I see others in miserable conditions or hear the wailing of any beings who are helplessly drowning in unbearable fear, I shall be able to rescue them from their fear.

All beings, regardless of whether they are physically close to me or distant, have all equally been my mother. Whenever I see or meet anyone, I shall be able to respect those who are older than me as my parents, those of the same age as my brothers or sisters, and those who are younger as my beloved sons or daughters. I shall be able to greet them respectfully. Whatever knowledge and understanding of Dharma I have, I shall sincerely and openly be able to offer it to my mother beings.

If I am truly concerned about the happiness of other fellow beings, then the lifelong practice of morality is crucial for me. It is impossible to accomplish the sincere benefit of others unless we can completely give up harming them verbally, physically, and even mentally. We forget the great instructions of Buddha as soon as someone harms us. We do not remember that he or she has been kind to us in the past and we generate harmful thoughts toward that person. This is how we begin to harm others. If we restrain ourselves from harming others, however, we not only achieve happy rebirths into many future lifetimes, we also benefit countless beings.

Whether I am alone or with others, I shall always be mindful and aware of my own thoughts, speech, and physical actions. Thus, I shall be able to maintain the pure practice of morality: positive speech, positive physical activities, and a positive mental attitude.

3. Meditation on the Perfection of Patience

The practice of patience is the pillar of the bodhisattvas' practice. Many of us are unable to accomplish our goal of benefiting others and this is only because we lack the strength of patience.

At the moment, although we have a sincere and good motivation to benefit others, our mental situation is not stable. When others respond positively, we are happy to help and benefit them. When we receive a negative response, however, we lose our positive attitude and become disheartened. We generate not only anguish and unhappiness within ourselves, but also thoughts of harming others. This impatient attitude not only deprives us of being able to benefit others, it also leads both ourselves and others through an endless cycle of unhappiness.

Whenever others harm me, I shall be able to remind myself of the fact that they have truly been my mother and have been kind to me. However, when they are harming me they are totally under the obsession of their inner delusions; their minds are too blind to distinguish what is right from what is wrong. They are like beloved ones possessed by an evil spirit and doing many harmful things to themselves and others. Therefore, instead of being angry, I shall be able to develop greater sympathy for them in order to free them from the cause of suffering.

Whenever I see or meet any fellow beings, I shall consider myself their sincere and humble servant, as the great noble-minded bodhisattvas do. Whether those around me behave in a friendly or unfriendly manner, I shall always be respectful to them. My great teacher, Buddha Shakyamuni, often taught:

Be always calm and peaceful. Do not be angry with others, even though they are angry with you. Do not retaliate, even though others hit you. Do not throw insults back, even though others insult you. Do not gossip about others, even though they slander you. Those who sincerely practice these four virtues are my spiritual Sons and Daughters.

I shall remind myself of this advice constantly, day and night.

4. Meditation on the Perfection of Enthusiastic Perseverance

Although I have obtained the precious human rebirth, through which even enlightenment can be attained within this very short lifetime, and although I have also met the stainless teachings of the Enlightened One and am able to meet many great spiritual friends, I have achieved almost nothing. The only reason for this is that I, on my part, lack the strength of enthusiastic perseverance in the practice of the great path that the bodhisattvas have traveled.

Since beginningless time I have been attached to only meaningless worldly pleasures and have thus failed to achieve any meaningful goals for myself, not to mention others. If I remain attached in this way, soon, when death comes, I will have no choice but to leave them all behind, however much I have achieved. I will have to travel again, alone, into the immeasurable suffering of the cycle of rebirth, without having gained anything meaningful. How much regret I would feel!

Now I have generated compassion toward all beings, dedicating myself to leading them to liberation from the sufferings of cyclic existence. How can I fulfill such a goal if I remain attached to these very temporary pleasures for myself alone? If I truly wish to achieve enlightenment for the sake of all my mother beings, I should not fool or deceive myself, but should constantly encourage myself to practice the meaningful activities of the Bodhisattvas' Path. Great bodhisattvas dedicate themselves to benefiting mother beings, by encouraging themselves thus:

I shall never lose courage, even if I need to remain in the great fire of hell for many eons to benefit my mother beings.

To lead others to true liberation from the sufferings of cyclic existence, we ourselves first need to be free from this suffering. The cause of all suffering is delusion; hence, we will not be able to liberate ourself from the suffering of cyclic existence unless and until our delusions are completely abandoned. What is the true antidote to all delusions? It is the wisdom that realizes the ultimate truth—the emptiness of inherent existence. To develop such pure wisdom, we need to cultivate and achieve the concentration of the single-pointed mind, the fully trained state of mind. Single-pointed mind and wisdom are the essential methods for achieving true liberation; therefore, I shall constantly develop these within myself with the pure motivation of wishing to benefit others.

O my great Guru Buddha Shakyamuni, please bestow the power of your compassion and wisdom upon me so that, through the practices of the six perfections, I will be able to achieve enlightenment for the sake of my mother beings.

After reflecting on the six perfections recite the following instructions by Atisha, written down by Geshe Chen Ngawa:

The Seven Points of Mind-Training

Accomplish first the training of your mind in the preliminary path [that is, the initial and medium levels of the path].

View that all phenomena are like a dream and penetrate into the unborn nature of your own mind. This remedy releases you from delusion.

View yourself as an illusory body before, during, and after meditation sessions and also during the break between sessions.

Meditate on giving and taking in an alternating way: put all the giving and taking on your outgoing and incoming breath, respectively.

There are three objects: [objects of pleasure, displeasure, and neutral objects]. There are three poisons: [desire or attachment, anger, and ignorance]. There are three virtues: [desirelessness, patience, and purity or wisdom].

Discipline or train your mind in all your behavior by reminding yourself of these instructional words.

When all the environment and inhabitants are filled with negativity, transform these adverse circumstances into the path to enlightenment.

Place all blame on your self-cherishing mind. Meditate on the kindness of others.

View the nature of your deluded mind as the four holy bodies (Sanskrit *kaya*): [(I) natural Dharmakaya, or emptiness; (2) wisdom Dharmakaya, or pure wisdom; (3) Sambhogakaya, or manifestation of pure wisdom in the original pure state of Buddha's body; (4) Nirmanakaya, or emanation of the Sambhogakaya in the form of the gross body]. The highest protection for yourself is meditation on emptiness.

Practice the four high methods: [accumulating merit by offering to your deity or guru, purifying your non-virtuous actions, giving offerings to evil spirits, and giving offerings to Dharma protectors].

Utilize every opportunity to meditate on bodhicitta.

Practice the five virtuous powers: [the power of determination, the power of familiarity, potential power produced through generating bodhicitta, the power of applying the antidote, and the power of prayer]. These five powers are methods of transferring [your consciousness to a higher rebirth] as taught in Mahayana instructions, therefore practice them with heedfulness. The essence of all Dharma lies in these practices.

Judge your practice through your experience and through the instructional words of others.

Always retain joyfulness in your own mind.

When you are able to control your mind even while you are not concentrating on a virtuous object, your mind is well-trained.

You should practice these three: [do not go against your own view or commitment; do not go against conventional behavior; do not practice mind-training in a discriminative way].

Change your attitude to a virtuous one but behave in a normal way.

Speak not of the physical faults of others.

Think not of any faults in others.

Give up all expectations, even expecting results from your virtuous practice.

Abandon poisoned food [that is, give up the self-cherishing mind].

Do not be too lenient in your attitude toward your own negativity.

Do not argue in a harsh way.

Do not plan to retaliate.

Do not humiliate anyone.

Do not load the ox with the load of a dzo [that is, do not place the blame for your own mistakes on others].

Do not rush to do things but do them properly.

Do not practice Dharma in the wrong way.

Do not invoke devas as evil spirits [that is, do not practice Dharma for your own selfish gain].

Do not seek wrong methods, which only bring misery, for the purpose of gaining pleasure.

Practice all meditation with one attitude—bodhicitta.

There are two things to be done, one at the beginning and one at the end: correct motivation and correct dedication.

Endure difficulties arising in both good and bad situations.

Guard your commitments as preciously as you guard your own life.

Practice these three difficulties: prevent delusions from arising; once a delusion does arise do not allow it to continue; try to eliminate delusions completely.

Practice the three principles: [rely on your guru; guard your mind; provide yourself with conducive conditions].

Practice not losing the three important things: [faith in the guru; enthusiasm in the practice of virtue; maintaining your commitments].

Do not separate your three doors [body, speech, and mind] from the three virtues. Maintain a virtuous attitude equally toward all beings.

Do not be so dependent upon external circumstances for happiness.

Do not waste this precious opportunity provided by the precious human rebirth.

Do not confuse virtue with non-virtue.

Do not practice mind-training inconsistently.

Practice Dharma with strong determination.

Practice Dharma without doubt.

First free your mind from whatever delusions predominate your mind.

Do not complain much.

Do not grumble.

Do not be moody.

Do not arrogantly repeat the good things you have done.

Thus, you should clearly understand the meaning of the mind-training teachings, which contain three essences: ultimate bodhicitta, or the wisdom realizing emptiness; conventional bodhicitta, or the altruistic mind; and the union of these two. These are likened to the sun, the wish-fulfilling tree, and the vajra respectively.

We should transform this unfortunate period, afflicted with the five negative conditions, into the path to enlightenment.

15. The Importance of Developing a Single-Pointed Mind, the Fifth Perfection

A single-pointed mind (Sanskrit *samatha*) is the fully trained state of the meditative mind; it serves as the ground for cultivating wisdom (Sanskrit *prajna*), which is the ultimate antidote to our delusions.

When we have achieved a single-pointed mind our mind is clear, calm, and stable. In that state we can analyze and penetrate deeply into any object of meditation and thus attain the pure realization of its true nature. This penetrative mind is called special insight (Sanskrit *vipaśyanā*), or wisdom—the two are synonymous. The difference between single-pointed mind and wisdom is that single-pointed mind has the ability to pacify our mind so that we can concentrate on the object of meditation, and wisdom has the special ability to analyze and penetrate into the subtle nature of the object of meditation. Thus, wisdom arises from a single-pointed mind. If we sincerely seek the realization of truth, therefore, we should first develop this clarity and strength of mind.

In his *Stages of Meditation* (Tibetan *Gom Rim*), the great yogi Kamalashila uses the analogy of a lamp to explain how wisdom arises from a single-pointed mind. When a candle is put in a place where there is no draft, it can illuminate everything around it clearly. Similarly, when our mind becomes clear and still, free from agitation and dullness, we are able to develop clear and deep insight into the true nature of the object we are meditating on.

Kamalashila also states:

If we solely practice developing a single-pointed mind and special insight, we will not only be able to liberate ourselves from the delusions that bind us to rebirth, but we will also be able to overcome the subtle imprints of delusions, the obstacles to the enlightened state.

Thus, whether we seek to liberate ourselves from the suffering of cyclic existence or seek the path to enlightenment, the essential methods lie only in the practices of developing a single-pointed mind and special insight.

All the virtuous qualities of arhats, who have completely reached beyond the cycle of rebirth, as well as the limitless excellent qualities of Tathagatas are the results of training their minds. Lord Buddha taught many techniques for training our mind to eliminate negative states and produce positive ones. These techniques are what is known as meditation. As we have discussed earlier, the Tibetan word for meditation, *gom*, means to familiarize our mind with virtuous states such as love, compassion, patience, and so on. Becoming familiar with such virtuous states is the only way to eliminate, or at least subdue, our deluded states of mind.

All the techniques for training our minds—whether sutra or tantra—are based on the practices of single-pointed mind and special insight. Buddha states clearly in the sutra called *Revealing the Thought of Buddha*:

> You should know that although I have taught many different aspects of the meditative states of Sravakas, bodhisattvas, and Tathagatas, these can all be included in the two practices of single-pointed mind and special insight.

In the same sutra Buddha tells how all the virtuous qualities we can gain are the result of single-pointed mind and special insight:

> Maitreya, all the virtuous qualities, both mundane and supramundane, that Sravakas and bodhisattvas gain and similarly, all the limitless qualities of the Tathagatas are the sole fruit of single-pointed mind and special insight.

Now let us see how the practices of single-pointed mind and special insight are essential methods to develop such virtuous qualities and eliminate all the negative or deluded states of mind such as anger, attachment, and so on. The only way to subdue and eventually eliminate our delusions is to develop a very strong virtuous state of mind as a direct antidote. The virtuous state of mind that enables us to eliminate our delusions arises solely from the realization of the ultimate truth, or the emptiness of the inherently existent self (see chapters 17 and 18). But until we are able to penetrate deeply into the nature of the object we are meditating on, we will not be able to realize the truth of that object. Shantideva says:

Having understood that only wisdom, which is firmly grounded on single-pointed mind, enables us to eliminate delusions from their root, we should first seek to develop single-pointed mind as the basis of wisdom.

Buddha Shakyamuni in meditation
(by the author)

16. How to Develop a Single-Pointed Mind

The practice of single-pointed mind is very important and useful because it is the only method for calming and stabilizing our mind. Without it we cannot gain any higher realizations through our meditation.

In the main part of this chapter we explain how to develop a single-pointed mind through nine stages as the method for achieving the fully trained state of single-pointed mind. This can only be done by following the practice of concentration based on these gradual steps over a long period of time as laid out here.

However, we can achieve some experience of single-pointed mind without accomplishing the nine stages. It is important to have some concentration for whatever subject we meditate on. Therefore, at the end of this chapter we explain short practical methods that help to develop some experience of single-pointed mind.

Buddha's instructions for developing a single-pointed mind are explained under three headings: (I) The prerequisites for developing a single-pointed mind; (II) The actual way of developing a single-pointed mind; (III) The result of practicing single-pointed mind.

I. The Prerequisites for Developing a Single-Pointed Mind

The prerequisite practices form the basis upon which we develop a single-pointed mind. Lord Buddha and subsequently many early Indian masters presented many different types of practice. Here we shall follow

Tsonghkapa's instructions, in which he condenses these practices into six: (A) abiding in a place conducive to developing a single-pointed mind; (B) controlling desire; (C) developing contentment; (D) giving up meaningless activities; (E) maintaining morality; (F) keeping our mind away from discursive thought.

What is a conducive place for developing single-pointed mind? In his *Ornament to the Sutras* Maitreya mentions five conditions: (1) it should not be difficult to obtain food and so on; (2) the environment should not be a danger to our life or health; (3) we should be close to where our spiritual teacher lives; (4) the surroundings should be quiet; (5) the atmosphere should be pleasant.

Abiding in a conducive place does not necessarily mean going to a remote place. We can create these conditions where we live and practice there.

Having created these conducive conditions, we should then check whether our mind is in a calm and clear state. It is very important to do this before starting the actual practice of single-pointed mind.

Desire, craving for material pleasure, and discursive thought—these are the main causes of distraction. Unless we at least minimize these, we will not be able to develop a single-pointed mind. If we find our mind is being influenced by desire or craving for material pleasures, we should reflect on the impermanent and suffering nature of our lives. If we have many discursive thoughts, we are instructed to do breathing meditation.

Many experienced Buddhist practitioners recommend breathing meditation as being a very effective method for controlling discursive thought. The obvious reason for this is that mind and inner psychic air are inseparably interrelated. Therefore, when we can pacify this inner air by meditating on the breath the mind naturally becomes still.

The Abhidharma scripture, Buddha's teachings on the nature of phenomena, mentions six steps in the meditation on the breath. The first one is simply to count our breath a certain number of times—say, twenty-five times. Once the mind becomes a little still we should go on to the second step, which is to watch the breathing. At this stage we are not counting the breath any more but simply watching the exhalation and inhalation of the breath. Do not conceptualize about it. All we have to do is observe the breath. The third step is not only watching the exhalation and inhalation of our breath, but also observing its rhythmic movement.

At the fourth step we observe the feelings and sensations accompanying the movement of the breath throughout the body. The fifth step is to analyze how the breath changes moment by moment, how it causes sensations and how these also change moment by moment. The last stage is called the stage of shifting. Here we shift from meditating on the breath to meditation on more profound and extensive objects, such as great compassion or the emptiness of self-existence.

Another important thing in the practice of single-pointed mind is keeping pure morality. Only through morality can we turn our minds away from the influence of gross delusions, which are caused by non-virtuous activities. Lama Tsonghkapa says:

> Of the six prerequisite practices, controlling discursive thought, maintaining pure morality, and inner quietness are the most important.

These practices are called causal grounds for developing a single-pointed mind because they provide all the necessary conditions for achieving it. Thus Tsonghkapa says:

> First we should strive to accomplish the six prerequisite practices, for when these are accomplished we can easily achieve a single-pointed mind.

Similarly, Atisha states in his *Lamp of the Path to Enlightenment*:

> If you do not have the prerequisite practices for developing a single-pointed mind you can spend one thousand years in meditation and still not achieve it.

II. The Actual Way of Developing a Single-Pointed Mind

The actual way of developing a single-pointed mind consists of three parts: (A) the posture; (B) the objects of meditation; (C) the actual way of developing concentration.

A. The Posture

When sitting in meditation there are seven aspects of the posture that we should keep in mind, as mentioned by Kamalashila: (1) sitting with legs crossed in the lotus position; (2) keeping the body upright; (3) keeping the shoulders straight and level, without any tension; (4) keeping the hands in the meditation posture; (5) pointing the eyes toward the tip of the nose in a relaxed way; (6) keeping the mouth in a normal position, not tightly closed or loosely open; (7) keeping the tongue against the palate.

This meditation posture was originally taught by Buddha in his tantric teachings, particularly in the yoga tantra called *The Enlightenment of Vairochana*. If, however, you find this position difficult you can sit in a comfortable position, keeping your back straight.

B. The Objects of Meditation

By objects of meditation we do not necessarily mean physical objects but something that we contemplate within our mind. They are classified into four types, as Tsonghkapa explains in his *Stages of the Path*. They are: (1) objects of meditation that pervade all objects of concentration and analysis; (2) objects to be meditated on for controlling delusion; (3) objects to be meditated on for developing insight; (4) objects to be meditated on for eliminating delusion. The first two are related to the practice of developing a single-pointed mind; the last two are specifically related to developing wisdom or special insight and are not explained here.

1. OBJECTS OF MEDITATION THAT PERVADE ALL OBJECTS OF CONCENTRATION AND ANALYSIS

All objects of meditation come into this category. Although there are many different types of meditational objects explained in both sutra and tantra teachings, all of them are either objects of concentration or analysis. This is why the first objects are called pervasive objects. In his *Stages of Meditation* Kamalashila classified them according to four aspects: (a) unanalyzed picture; (b) analyzed picture; (c) final nature of phenomena; (d) accomplished object.

(a) Unanalyzed Picture

This refers to the object that we use to develop concentration. When we develop concentration, we first need to build a clear picture of the object we are meditating on. Once such a picture is built in our mind, we place the mind on it and concentrate without analyzing it. For this reason Kamalashila called it unanalyzed picture.

(b) Analyzed Picture

When true single-pointed mind is achieved through developing concentration on the unanalyzed picture, the next stage is for us to develop special insight so that we can come to understand the ultimate nature of the object.

The proper way to develop special insight is to analyze the nature of the object we meditate on with concentration. This means that we are not only keeping the mind on the picture of the object we have built, but are analyzing the characteristics or aspects of that object. For this reason the object for developing special insight is called analyzed picture.

(c) Final Nature of Phenomena

The final nature of phenomena refers to their ultimate nature, or emptiness of self-existence.

According to Kamalashila's system, we first concentrate on the picture of the Buddha we have built in our mind, as he recommended. When we have achieved true single-pointed mind, we are then led to analyze the characteristics or aspects of that object, such as its color and shape. This leads us to gain penetrative insight. Once we are able to analyze the object while concentrating on the mental picture of it, we are then led to develop special insight into the ultimate nature of phenomena.

(d) Accomplished Object

The accomplished object defines that which is gained from developing special insight into the ultimate nature of phenomena. The final result or achievement of this practice is complete liberation from delusions, together with their subtle imprints; this is what is known as the Dharmakaya state, or enlightenment.

2. Objects of Meditation
for Controlling Delusion

The second type of objects of meditation are objects to develop a virtuous mind, such as love or impermanence, and are taught for the purpose of controlling the delusions that mostly disturb our minds. For example, some people have more problems with anger, while others have more problems with desire, jealousy, or attachment. We should try to control the delusion that disturbs us most. So we should practice meditation on specific virtuous objects that directly counteract that particular delusion. In his *Great Exposition of the Stages of the Path* Tsonghkapa presented five different objects of meditation: (a) meditation on ugliness as the antidote to attachment; (b) meditation on love as the antidote to anger; (c) meditation on the interdependent origination of the twelve links as the antidote to ignorance; (d) meditation on breathing as the antidote to discursive thought; (e) meditation on analysis of the six elements as the antidote to pride.

The essential thing here is that we first check up on what kind of delusion mostly agitates our minds. If, for example, we find our problem is anger, then we should concentrate on controlling our anger by meditating on love. If our problem is mostly due to pride, then we should meditate on the analysis of the six elements.

Let us discuss a little how to meditate on these five objects.

(a) Meditation on Ugliness as the Antidote to Attachment

Meditating on the ugliness of our body and environment is a very powerful way to subdue our desire and attachment to material pleasures. Vasubandhu mentioned three stages of this meditation in his *Treasury of Knowledge*.

First we should visualize a piece of bone the size of our fingernail, in between our eyebrows, and focus on it for a while. The bone multiplies from one into countless bones, completely covering our body and then gradually covering the whole earth. The bones that cover the whole earth then gradually dissolve back into the bones covering our body. Here we stop and repeat the process. This is called the beginners' stage.

Once we can do this visualization clearly and without interruption, we move to the second stage. Again visualize the bone as small as your fingernail in between your eyebrows, and spread it by multiplying it from one bone into countless bones, until the whole earth is covered by countless bones. Then they gradually dissolve back to the bones on our body, then to the pieces of bone that cover our forehead and we focus on them. We should repeat this visualization until we gain clarity and stability in the visualization.

At the third stage the visualization is the same as the previous one, except here we dissolve the bones back to the original one that was visualized in between the eyebrows. Again we should continue with this meditation until we have gained a stable and clear visualization of this process.

(b) Meditation on Love as the Antidote to Anger
Meditation on love is the same as explained in the practice of bodhicitta (see pages 107–09).

(c) Meditation on the Twelve Links of Interdependent Origination as the Antidote to Ignorance
Meditation on the twelve links of interdependent origination is the antidote to ignorance. Ignorance, here, means our misconceptions of suffering and the cause of suffering. Teachings on the twelve links of interdependent origination profoundly and lucidly show how delusion and karma lead to rebirth, and thus how our lives are in the nature of suffering; they also show what the cause of suffering is. Whenever we do not understand suffering and the cause of suffering we should meditate on this teaching (see page 94–96).

(d) Meditation on Breathing as the Antidote to Discursive Thought
The fourth object, the antidote to discursive thought, is meditation on breathing. This is explained on page 172–73.

(e) Meditation on Analysis of the Six Elements as the Antidote to Pride
The fifth meditation is an analysis of the six elements. Many experienced yogis admire this meditation as an effective way of controlling pride. The main cause of pride is clinging to the sense of ego or "I," holding it to be a concrete entity. When you analyze yourself, breaking yourself down into many individual constituent elements, the feeling of a concrete self begins to diminish. Thus this meditation enables us to subdue, or at least reduce, any kind of pride that hinders our minds from being calm or still.

Tsonghkapa mentioned two ways of meditating on the six elements. In the first one, the aggregates upon which the "I" or ego is imputed is broken into six parts. First look at how the "I" exists. We will clearly see that the "I" or self is something that is composed of many constituent elements. Then we mentally separate these elements into the six types: earth, water, fire, air, space, and consciousness. We observe how these six elements function and how each one differs from the others in its characteristics.

The second way is that we observe how the six elements are related to each other to form the aggregation upon which the "I" is imputed. We think that the "I" no longer exists in any concrete form, but exists as a mere label on the basis of the aggregates.

C. The Actual Way of Developing Concentration

The very first step is to establish the object we are going to concentrate on. This means building a clear image or picture of the object of meditation—for instance, the form of Buddha or whatever we have chosen. Actually many yogis recommend that we take the form of Buddha for developing concentration. We should try to build the image of the object until we are able to visualize it clearly. Once the visualization becomes clear and stable, we should then place the mind on it and concentrate. While we are concentrating, it is very important to keep the mind clear and alert. Many yogis say that this is as important as maintaining our concentration.

The main purpose of developing a single-pointed mind is to gain deep realization into the ultimate truth. But in order to realize the subtle nature of an object such as emptiness, it is not sufficient just to be able to concentrate. More importantly, our mind must be alert and lucid so that it can analyze and penetrate into the subtle nature of the object with great agility.

The main obstacle to maintaining alertness of mind is mental dullness. This happens when our attention to the object loses its intensity. Tsonghkapa classified two levels of dullness: gross and subtle. When gross mental dullness arises in the mind, there is no longer clarity, so the mind becomes sluggish. This is quite easy to recognize. However, when subtle mental dullness arises, there is still clarity—the mind can still see the object clearly. Tsonghkapa says that this is very difficult to recognize and can easily be confused with true single-pointed mind.

The difference between subtle dullness and true single-pointed mind is that although there is clarity in subtle dullness, our attention is no longer so intensive and the mind sinks a little. Whenever this happens we must be aware of it, elevate the mind and rebuild strong attention. But if we are too concerned about building attention this often causes the mind to wander from the object; on the other hand, if we do not make an effort to keep hold of the visualization with intensive attention, then the mind begins to sink. For this reason Master Chandragomin says:

> If we do not make the effort to build intensive attention, the mind will begin to sink and we will never be able to achieve alertness. On the other hand, if we place too much emphasis on maintaining intensive attention, this causes the mind to wander from the object and we will never be able to achieve stability. Hence it is not easy to keep to the middle way when developing a single-pointed mind.

How should the meditator deal with this problem? Tsonghkapa says that when we begin to practice concentration, it is more or less inevitable for the mind to sink or become distracted. Therefore in the beginning we should concentrate for very short lengths of time, taking breaks and concentrating again. This method helps us maintain both stability and alertness. Later, as our practice improves, we can try concentrating for longer periods. Tsonghkapa always stresses how important it is to stop concentrating before we actually get tired.

Now we will focus on the hindrances to maintaining stability of mind when practicing concentration. There are two main obstacles, namely wandering thoughts and distraction.

Wandering thoughts are undisciplined thoughts that move from one object to another. Unless these are overcome, it is very difficult to still the mind. We can overcome them by developing awareness and mindfulness. Whenever our mind wanders from the meditation object, we must be aware of it and bring it back to the object. We should discipline our mind in this way and so develop stability of mind.

The second obstacle, distraction, is mainly caused by desire and attachment to the pleasures of this life. When we find that we are being distracted in this way, we should meditate on the suffering nature of cyclic existence and impermanence.

The actual way of developing concentration is explained in three stages: (1) how to develop the eight positive states of mind as antidotes to the five defects; (2) how to develop concentration through nine stages; (3) reliance on the six powers.

1. How to Develop the Eight Positive States of Mind as Antidotes to the Five Defects

These are mentioned by Maitreya in his text *Distinguishing the Middle Way from the Extremes*. The five defects are: (a) laziness; (b) forgetfulness; (c) mental dullness and distraction; (d) not applying the antidote when obstacles arise; (e) attempting to apply the antidote when there is no obstacle.

The eight antidotes to these are: (a) faith; (b) aspiration; (c) enthusiasm; (d) suppleness; (e) mindfulness; (f) awareness; (g) application of the antidote; (h) equilibrium.

(a) Laziness

Laziness is a lack of interest in our virtuous activities and as long as we are influenced by it we will not have much desire or energy to practice developing a single-pointed mind. This is the result of being attached to material pleasures or meaningless activities such as gambling. When we are attached to these we lose all interest in practicing any kind of virtuous path. So it is essential to overcome this unwholesome attitude if we want to attain single-pointed mind.

What is the antidote to this defect? Mental suppleness is the antidote to laziness. When our mind is completely supple, we can concentrate on any given virtuous object whenever we want to, for as long as we wish and without any physical or mental discomfort. What is more, it is accompanied by great joy and tremendous enthusiasm.

How do we develop these excellent qualities of suppleness? Maitreya says that mental suppleness arises from enthusiasm. This in turn arises from aspiration. The basis of aspiration is faith. Therefore we need to develop strong faith in the single-pointed mind. Unless we can see the benefits and advantages of achieving such a mind, we will not be able to generate faith in it. So we should remind ourselves of its excellent qualities and many good results. Once we are convinced of these we will have faith and naturally aspire to achieve a single-pointed mind. From this aspiration, enthusiasm automatically arises.

(b) Forgetfulness

This means forgetting the instructions we have received from our spiritual teacher. It is very important when developing a single-pointed mind to be able to remember all the details of instruction, so that we can practice accurately and apply the right antidote when obstacles arise. Mindfulness is the antidote here.

(c) Mental Dullness and Distraction

These are the main obstacles that arise when we practice a single-pointed mind. The antidote to both is awareness, for we need to be aware whenever they arise and then try to abandon them.

When we first practice we will find distraction the greatest problem. Our mind will wander away from the object of meditation, so we must become aware of it, gently bring the mind back, and continue concentrating. If the distraction is very strong, we should stop concentrating for a while and try to abandon the cause. As mental distraction is usually caused by meaningless activities, experienced yogis suggest that we meditate on the impermanence of our lives and the suffering nature of cyclic existence. This helps subdue our desire or attachment to worldly pleasures and so overcome distraction.

At a later stage, when our concentration improves, we will find our mind beginning to sink or become dull. We are advised to elevate it and make it joyful by reflecting on the value of having found this precious human rebirth or by remembering the excellent qualities of buddhas and bodhisattvas (see page 76). In his *Compendium of Knowledge* Asanga suggests that we visualize a pinpoint of white light in between our eyebrows, radiating into the ten directions. This helps clear the mind of dullness.

Tsonghkapa repeatedly stressed the importance of keeping our mind fresh and alert while we are practicing concentration. For this it is essential to have continual awareness and not be lazy about dealing with dullness and distraction whenever they appear.

Chandragomin says:

If the elephant of our mind is tightly tied to the post of awareness
with the rope of mindfulness, then we can easily tame it.

To be able to detect mental dullness and distraction the moment they arise,
we also need to have strong mindfulness. In this respect mindfulness does
not mean remembering the instructions; it is the power to hold the object
in our mind while concentrating on it. If there is not enough mindfulness, we can easily lose the object, so maintaining mindfulness is crucial in
this practice. In this way, then, mindfulness is likened to the rope with
which the crazy elephant is tied to the post.

There are many techniques in this practice that teach us how to develop
mindfulness. For example, while concentrating, we should be alert so that
we can easily be aware of whether our mind is focusing on the object or
drifting away from it. Thus awareness helps to develop mindfulness. Also,
Tsonghkapa advises that before we start concentrating, we should think
with strong determination, "I will concentrate on this object for such and
such a period of time and I will not let my mind wander away from it."
This motivation can help us hold the object.

It is very important to be able to deal with the two main obstacles to
developing concentration. First we have to recognize them, we have to be
aware of them, on the alert. For this reason, awareness is said to be the antidote to dullness and distraction.

(d) Not Applying the Antidote when Obstacles Arise

This is a type of laziness. Sometimes we notice the obstacles as they arise,
but remain careless and do nothing about them. This laziness can be a
great hindrance, therefore we should be very heedful and get rid of obstacles as soon as we are aware of them.

(e) Attempting to Apply the Antidote when There is no Obstacle

This can happen when we place too much emphasis on applying the antidote, which makes us feel anxious about it. We check up on whether obstacles are arising in our mind, when there is no need to do so. Therefore,
when we are concentrating well, we should not be anxious to see if obstacles are arising; we should just carry on in a relaxed way, without checking.
This relaxation is called equilibrium.

2. How to Develop Concentration through Nine Stages

In his *Ornament to the Sutras* Maitreya explains how to develop concentration through the nine stages. They are:

1 Inwardly placing the mind on the chosen object.
2 Extending the duration of concentration on the object.
3 Replacing the mind on the object when it is distracted.
4 Continuously replacing the mind on the object when distracted.
5 Disciplining the mind.
6 Pacifying the mind.
7 Fully pacifying the mind.
8 Single-pointed mind.
9 Equilibrium.

When we can easily turn our mind toward the chosen object and concentrate on it for a little while, we have reached the first stage. However, we cannot keep our mind on the object very easily.

As our concentration improves a little, we can keep the mind on the object quite easily and for a little longer; this is the second stage. Although we can concentrate for a while, we cannot bring our mind back to the object very easily when we are distracted.

At the third stage, not only can we concentrate a little longer, but we find it easier to bring the mind back to the object when distracted.

At the fourth stage, our awareness has been improved and we are able to bring the mind back to the object without difficulty.

At the fifth stage, our mind is well disciplined in that we are mostly able to concentrate whenever we like and for as long as we want, without much interruption caused by distraction or dullness. However, we do not yet feel confident about concentrating without being cautious; our mind can still be influenced by subtle discursive thought and subtle dullness.

Therefore, from this stage onward, we emphasize mindfulness and awareness, so that we can prevent the mind from being influenced by any obstacles. As a result of this we achieve great mental tranquility; this is the sixth stage.

When this tranquility becomes stable we have reached the seventh stage. On the basis of this stable tranquility we can improve our concentration enormously.

At the eighth stage we are able to concentrate on the object for as long as we wish without any disturbance, not even subtle dullness or subtle distraction. But we still need to rely on a little effort to be able to concentrate.

When we reach the ninth stage we no longer need to depend on any effort to concentrate on the object. Having reached this stage we will soon achieve full mental and physical suppleness, accompanied by great joy. Then we will have fully achieved a single-pointed state of mind.

3. RELIANCE ON THE SIX POWERS

In order to improve our concentration through the nine stages, we need to rely on the special method of the six powers and four awarenesses. The six powers are as follows:

1 The power of instruction.
2 The power of contemplation.
3 The power of mindfulness.
4 The power of alertness.
5 The power of enthusiasm.
6 The power of familiarization.

Let us see how these powers are related to the nine stages: At the first stage the power of instruction is very important. We have to remember and keep to all the instructions that our spiritual guide has given us on developing concentration. Since we do not have much experience of concentration at this stage, we happily rely on these instructions.

At the second stage we have some experience of concentration, so it is important to emphasize our own experience of contemplation. By deepening our contemplation, we can effectively improve our concentration.

At the third stage we are still often distracted, even though we can concentrate for a while. Therefore we have to learn how to bring the mind back to the object and for this we need mindfulness.

From the fourth to the sixth stage, the main obstacles are subtle dullness and subtle distraction. Therefore at these three stages we place more emphasis on developing deep alertness, so that we can detect these obstacles as soon as they arise.

When we reach the seventh stage there is not much disturbance, not even from subtle dullness and subtle distraction, but we still rely on effort until we reach the ninth stage. Therefore at the seventh and eighth stages the most important thing to develop is joyful enthusiasm so that we can concentrate without any discomfort. If we do lose enthusiasm at these stages we could become distracted by subtle dullness or subtle discursive thought. So the power of enthusiasm also keeps these subtle disturbances at bay.

At the ninth stage we achieve the full power to be able to concentrate without any interruption or effort. Therefore at this stage we just concentrate in a relaxed way, without any anxiety. This is the power of familiarization.

There are four kinds of awareness that we achieve at the different stages of concentration. They are:

1   awareness with effort
2   continual awareness
3   uninterrupted awareness
4   effortless awareness.

At the first two of the nine stages, awareness with effort is important because during these two stages our concentration relies on constant effort. Once we reach the third stage we gain the ability to concentrate uninterruptedly for longer without relying on constant effort. Therefore from the third to the seventh stage we use continual awareness. At the eighth stage we have uninterrupted awareness since we can concentrate without interruptions. And at the last stage we no longer need to rely on any effort to concentrate; thus this is called effortless awareness.

III. The Result of Practicing Single-Pointed Mind

By developing the six powers and four awarenesses through the nine stages of concentration, we will be able to concentrate on the object without any effort, with alertness and inexhaustible suppleness and for as long as we want; this is true single-pointed mind, or samatha.

Samatha is a Sanskrit word, translated into Tibetan as *zhinay*. *Zhi* means to pacify and *nay* means to remain still or abide in. These words clearly reflect the distinctive features of true samatha: a highly trained state of mind, free from any kind of disturbance, enabling us to concentrate on any chosen object for as long as we wish.

The great Lama Tsonghkapa explained the two distinctive qualities of the single-pointed mind as follows: alertness and the pacification of any obstacles that can cause the mind to become either dull or distracted. Pacification leads to stability and clarity, for when distractions are pacified the mind becomes stable and when dullness is removed the mind always remains clear. The first quality, alertness, signifies suppleness—a very important quality of the single-pointed mind.

In his analogy of the lamp, Kamalashila beautifully illustrates how a single-pointed mind provides clarity and stillness as the foundation for developing insight, so that we can penetrate into the ultimate nature of things. The candle illuminates everything around it clearly when there is no disturbance from the wind, that is, when it burns calmly. This not only describes the qualities of a single-pointed mind but also shows how it serves as a sound basis on which sharp and deep insight can easily be developed.

To realize the ultimate truth it is not sufficient to be able to concentrate; the mind must be so supple that it can analyze its object in any way it wants. This is why we need to develop all the qualities of a single-pointed mind.

How to Develop a Single-Pointed Mind in Daily Sessions

So far we have discussed how to develop the fully trained state of single-pointed mind based on a long-term practice in gradual stages. Now we shall explain short, practical methods for developing some experience of single-pointed mind, which can be practiced in short, daily sessions.

Sit on a comfortable cushion in meditation posture as explained on page 174 and then contemplate taking refuge and developing bodhicitta. Having done this we visualize the merit field in front of us and perform the Seven Limb Prayer and mandala offering.

Now we start the actual practice of meditation, which is in two stages: relaxing our body and mind and developing concentration.

It is important to be relaxed when developing a single-pointed mind, therefore experienced yogis suggest that we do a breathing exercise before we start meditating. Here we visualize the three psychic channels within our body, through which wind energy moves (see the following page).

As we grow up the central channel usually becomes blocked and wind energy moves only through the left and right channels. There are special techniques to send wind energy through the central channel and when this happens it flows very gently so that the mind becomes calm and clear. One of these techniques is this breathing exercise, which has three stages: (1) visualizing the three channels, (2) cleansing them, and (3) holding the breath in the central channel.

We begin by visualizing the three channels: they start between the eyebrows, go up to the crown of the head just inside the skull. From there they bend straight down, quite close to the spinal cord, right down to the sex organ, ending close to the top of the central part in the male organ and close to the opening of the female organ. The channels are as thick as a drinking straw but very fine, smooth, flexible, and luminous and open at both ends. The central channel is blue, the right one is red, and the left is white.

Having visualized the channels we now come to cleansing them. As we grow up many defects can occur in different places in the channels and unless we cleanse them the energy cannot flow gently.

We begin by visualizing the left and right channels connected at the sex organ, not open as in their original position. Then we take a long breath through the right nostril, sending the breath all the way along the right channel down to the sex organ. The breath comes up through the left channel, expelling all impurities through the left nostril. This is repeated three times.

Breathing in through the left nostril, send the air down the left channel; then up the right one while breathing out and expelling all the impurities that were inside it. This is also repeated three times.

Finally visualize the ends of the two side channels tucked into the central channel at the sex organ. Breathing in simultaneously through both the right and left nostrils, we send the air down the side channels; then up into the central channel while breathing out and expelling all the impurities through both nostrils. Do this three times. Then visualize that the three channels are perfectly clean and luminous.

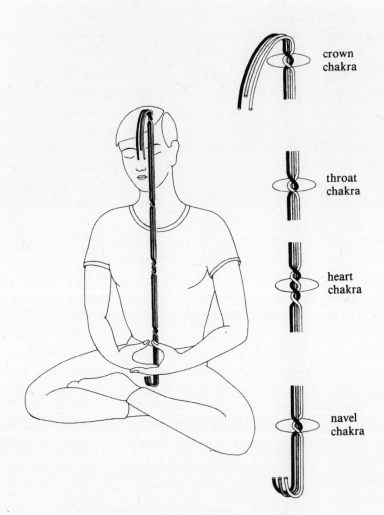

crown
chakra

throat
chakra

heart
chakra

navel
chakra

The three main psychic channels, showing the main chakras

We now come to the third stage: holding the breath in the central channel. Imagine that the ends of the two side channels are taken out of the central channel and put back in their original position. Now the central channel is open so that wind energy can move through it without going through the side channels.

When we breathe in, the breath or wind energy spreads throughout the body. Here, just before we breathe out, visualize the breath energies coming from the lower part of your body up to the bottom of the central channel. From there they enter into the central channel and remain inside it at the level of the navel. Concentrate briefly, still holding the breath.

Then breathe in more deeply, visualizing all the upper part of the breath energies entering into the central channel through the opening between the eyebrows, moving gently down to the level of the navel. Then hold both breaths—the breath that comes from the lower part of your body and the breath you have just breathed in—and visualize them remaining inside the central channel at the navel in the form of a small ball of energy and concentrate on it.

Then gently breathe out, visualizing wind energy moving back from your central channel throughout your body. This can be done a few times. When you feel your mind become calm and clear, concentrate on mental clarity and calmness without any thoughts.

This breathing exercise helps us to relax our physical energy and mind. On the basis of this we practice the actual meditation, developing a single-pointed mind. First we fix the object of concentration, then simply keep the mind single-pointedly on it with alertness and mindfulness. Buddhist scriptures mention three different types of object for developing concentration: we can either visualize (1) a clear picture of Buddha or a bodhisattva, (2) a tiny point of light, the size of a sesame seed, at a certain level within the central channel, or (3) we can meditate on the clarity of our own mind.

There are six important places or chakras within the central channel: between the eyebrows, just below the crown of the head, and at the level of the throat, heart, navel, and sex organ. We can visualize the tiny, luminous, clear point of light at any of these places. Generally, however, experienced Buddhist yogis advise us to visualize the point of light between our eyebrows or at our crown chakra if we tend to experience dullness. If our mind tends to become distracted or wanders, then visualize the point of light at the level of our navel or sex organ.

If we want to develop a single-pointed mind by concentrating on the clarity of our own mind, we should first wholeheartedly request Guru Shakyamuni to bestow his blessings upon us so that we may instantly recognize the luminous nature of our own mind and then maintain our concentration on it. Soon after this request is made, visualize that a second emanation of Guru Shakyamuni emerges from the one residing at the center of the merit field and dissolves into our own mind. As soon as this happens, all our discursive thoughts suddenly cease and the luminous nature of our own mind manifests. At this point we should not recall past thoughts or anticipate any new ones. We should simply let a part of our mind watch, with constant mindfulness and alertness, the luminous nature of our mind that we are experiencing at that moment.

To be able to maintain concentration it is most important to develop strong and constant attention on the luminous nature of our mind, without allowing it to follow any discursive thoughts. Whenever a new thought arises our concentration is normally taken over or simply swept away by it—this is the main obstacle to controlling discursive thought. If we are able to develop our attention on the inner luminous nature of our mind, though some thoughts may still arise, they cannot distract our attention and will of themselves cease. In this way we can continuously maintain concentration on the luminous nature of our mind.

In all cases—whether the object of our concentration is a mental picture of Buddha, the tiny point of light within our psychic channel or the luminous nature of our mind—the main obstacles to developing a single-pointed mind are dullness and distraction. We should familiarize ourselves with the antidotes to these, as explained on pages 178–82, and apply them when necessary.

Tsonghkapa suggests that in the beginning it is better to meditate on single-pointed mind for short periods—say twenty minutes—and as we advance we can prolong our sessions for up to one or two hours. Whatever we choose as our object of concentration, we should maintain our concentration with constant mindfulness and alertness.

At the end of the session visualize clear light together with nectar emerging from the heart of Guru Buddha Shakyamuni and the great bodhisattvas within the merit field. The light and nectar dissolve into our body through the crown chakra, purifying our mind of all obstacles to the single-pointed mind.

Nagarjuna

17. The Wisdom of Emptiness, the Sixth Perfection

The Lineage of the Teachings on the Truth of Emptiness

The fully awakened clear state of mind that realizes the truth of emptiness—the emptiness of inherent existence—is the wisdom we seek. It is called *prajna* in Sanskrit. When we achieve this wisdom we are able to realize emptiness from the depth of our own personal experience, beyond intellectualization.

This wisdom alone has the true power to cut our delusions from their root completely. No matter how many other virtuous qualities we may have, there is no way to achieve the complete elimination of our delusions unless and until the full realization of emptiness is gained. Therefore, whether we seek liberation or enlightenment, it is essential for us to seek this wisdom.

To gain the full realization of emptiness we must necessarily have developed our inner understanding to the point where we can fully negate the inherently existent self, yet at the same time not fail to maintain the conventional reality of the self—the truth that self does exist in general. This is the perfect middle way of understanding emptiness, as taught by Buddha and elaborated by Master Nagarjuna, who established the Madhyamika or Middle Way School, some four hundred years after Buddha had passed away.

We cannot gain the full realization of emptiness without a foundation, hence Buddha taught the emptiness of the substantially existent self and the emptiness of the externally existent self as a basis for understanding the most subtle emptiness—the emptiness of inherent existence.

Among the followers of Buddha's teachings on emptiness there arose four different lineage-holders of his teachings on emptiness, known as the four Buddhist schools: Vaibashika (followers of the early commentaries— *The Mahavibhasa*—on the sutras); Sautrantika (Sutra Citers); Cittamatra (Mind Only); and Madhyamika (The Middle Way).

The Vaibashika and Sautrantika Schools mainly follow Buddha's teachings on the emptiness of the substantially existent self. These two schools view the emptiness of the substantially existent self to be the highest form of emptiness that Buddha taught. The Vaibashika School was founded by the early Buddhist masters such as Vasumitra, Gosaka, and Buddhadeva. The Sautrantika School was founded by Master Guma-Rata and Sri Rata. Both schools were founded before Nagarjuna established the Madhyamika School and equally follow Buddha's teachings on the emptiness of the substantially existent self. However, the difference between them is that the Vaibashikas rely on commentaries written by early masters, whereas the Sautrantikas strictly follow the sutras, the words of Buddha himself.

The Cittamatra School views the emptiness of the externally existent self to be the highest form of emptiness that Buddha taught. This school was established by Master Asanga not long after Nagarjuna founded the Madhyamika School.

The Madhyamika School holds the view that the emptiness of the inherently existent self is the highest form of emptiness that Buddha taught. The ultimate aim of the Buddha is to lead us to the full realization of the most subtle emptiness—the emptiness of inherent existence as elaborated by Nagarjuna. The first two forms of emptiness, the emptiness of the substantially existent self and the emptiness of the externally existent self, are taught as steps toward the full understanding of the most subtle emptiness.

Nagarjuna established the Madhyamika School by extensively teaching the emptiness of inherent existence, as taught by Buddha in the *Perfection Sutras*. Buddha himself prophesied:

A great yogi called Nagarjuna will come four hundred years after I pass away to revive my teachings on emptiness purely, by dispelling the two extremes of nihilism and eternalism.

As Buddha prophesied, Nagarjuna refuted all mistaken views on emptiness and purely revived Buddha's teachings on emptiness. Many yogis and scholars such as Buddhapalita, Nagarbodhi, Chandrakirti, Shantideva, Naropa, and Atisha, as well as the early Tibetan Buddhist yogis and scholars, followed his explanations on emptiness.

The great Tsonghkapa strictly followed the teachings on emptiness established by Nagarjuna and elaborated by his two chief disciples—Buddhapalita and Chandrakirti. Once, Tsonghkapa asked Manjushri:

Nagarjuna had many outstanding disciples who wrote great treatises. Who can I rely on most in order to gain the stainless realization of emptiness?

Manjushri answered:

Yes, Nagarjuna had many distinguished disciples, but in their understanding of his view you should follow Buddhapalita and in particular, Chandrakirti. Chandrakirti was a great bodhisattva, the chief disciple of Lord Buddha in the pure land called Limitless Light, just before he took rebirth on earth as Chandrakirti. He had prayed to be born here to be able to pass on the pure teachings on emptiness, according to Nagarjuna's view. You can fully rely on his teachings on the most profound and subtle aspects of both sutra and tantra practice as taught by Buddha.

Atisha clearly said that Chandrakirti was able to meet Nagarjuna (who lived for six hundred years) and received many teachings directly from him. Buddhapalita and Chandrakirti are held to be the two distinguished moon and sun-like disciples of Nagarjuna. Chandrakirti lived later than Buddhapalita and some Tibetan scholars believe that Chandrakirti was the re-incarnation of Buddhapalita. It is said in the life-story of Atisha, who lived in the eleventh century, that when a Tibetan scholar called Nagtso went to India to invite Atisha to Tibet, he saw an old, highly respected yogi sitting in the top row of monks at Atisha's monastery, Vikramashila, and thought it must be Atisha. Later, he was told that it was not Atisha but a chief disciple of Chandrakirti called Rigpey Khujug. This story shows that Chandrakirti lived not long before Atisha.

The Importance of Seeking
the Truth of Emptiness

The truth of emptiness is the essence of all Buddha's teachings. The realization of this truth is not only the ultimate method for us to cut our own delusions from their root, but is also the key path that leads us to the perfect state of Buddhahood. It is important to cut our delusions if we truly wish to be liberated from the suffering of samsara, not to mention how important it is for us to control and eliminate our own delusions to be able to help others effectively and in a sincere and pure way. Hence, as Buddha says in the *Perfection Sutras*:

> The wisdom that realizes the emptiness of the inherently existent self is the mother of both those who reach beyond the suffering of cyclic existence for their own peace and those who attain enlightenment for the sake of all beings.

Similarly Chandrakirti points out:

> All those who go beyond cyclic existence have attained their liberation through the perfect teachings of the Enlightened Ones. These are born from bodhisattvas who fully develop themselves to benefit others. Bodhisattvas in turn are born from three seeds only: the realization of emptiness, the mind of enlightenment, and great compassion.

If we look at the origin of our anger, attachment, and so on, we can clearly see from our own experience that they arise from our misconception of self, holding the view that the "I" exists inherently. Thus it is clear why only the realization of emptiness has the power to cut our delusions completely. No matter how much and for how long we might concentrate on developing the practice of other virtuous paths, such as single-pointed mind, morality, patience, and so on, we will not be able to eliminate our delusions unless and until the truth of emptiness is correctly realized. Here Tsonghkapa says:

Cultivating other antidotes to delusions, for example, developing patience as the antidote to anger or frustration and developing a single-pointed mind as the antidote to discursive thought, is like cutting a branch off a poisonous tree. However, developing the realization of the truth of emptiness as the antidote to our delusions is like cutting the poisonous tree at the root.

Therefore, we should be so happy to seek the faultless meaning of emptiness as presented by the great yogis Nagarjuna, Chandrakirti, and Lama Tsonghkapa. Unless we are mindless we cannot neglect these teachings. How fortunate we are to have this rare opportunity to receive and practice them. These precious teachings even enable us to become enlightened in one lifetime. Let us make a sincere effort on our part to practice them.

Understanding Emptiness According to the Middle Way

The pure understanding of emptiness as taught by Buddha and elaborated by the great Nagarjuna and subsequently by his two main disciples, Buddhapalita and Chandrakirti, is the understanding of emptiness according to the middle way: completely negating the inherently existent self while maintaining the existence of the self that is commonly known to everyone without damaging it. This realization is what Lama Tsonghkapa called the union of the two truths. This means that although our self lacks an inherently existent nature, it nevertheless exists and carries out activities, good actions leading to happiness and bad actions leading to unhappiness. Each and every thing that exists has two natures: an ultimate nature and a conventional nature. By understanding the ultimate nature we can get rid of our deeply ingrained misconception of the things we perceive and experience; by understanding the conventional nature we have no trouble understanding the law of cause and effect.

It is most important that we differentiate between which kind of self should be negated and which should be maintained. If we negate too much, we will find it difficult to maintain the self that is commonly known to us and that is the basis of our identification. If we negate this normal self, we will have problems in maintaining our understanding of the law of cause and effect. We will see no point in virtuous actions and not understand that our suffering is the result of past non-virtuous actions. This is the extreme of nihilism.

For those who truly wish to understand the root of suffering and how to get rid of suffering, it is very important to maintain the self that is responsible for happiness and unhappiness. This self cannot be reduced to our material body; it is more than this. It is something that comes from our past lives and goes on to the next life. Seeing this, we can understand that the suffering we experience does not come from outside, but is a consequence of our previous karma. Happiness also comes from past lives. Our virtuous actions of this life can lead to happiness in our next life. Our practice of Dharma can eventually lead us to enlightenment.

However, when we come to establish that the self is not something limited to our material body but comes from past lives and goes to the next life, some people—non-Buddhist masters, for example—go to the extreme of eternalism. They believe that the self exists independently and eternally. On the one hand this belief helps to maintain our understanding of karma; on the other hand, however, it strengthens our self-grasping because it views the self as something solid. This leads us to cling to our self, thus keeping us bound to the sufferings of cyclic existence.

Therefore Buddha taught the middle way: that self is not limited to this very material body, but comes from our past life and goes on to the next. It does not exist solidly but is something merely imputed or labeled by our mind on the basis of the aggregates of which we are composed (see page 206).

If we do not negate enough then we will not be able to negate the inherently existent self to which the mind clings. As a result we will not be able to eliminate our delusions.

When we try to negate the inherent self without recognizing it properly through our own experience, we feel afraid to attempt to refute it. This is because we fear that the existence of the commonly known self will be negated altogether. Under this condition we try to negate only the very gross form of the inherently existent self: for example, the self seen as eternal, as a solid, separate entity, independent of the body and mind. When we are angry we have this view of the self. By negating this we can overcome the most gross form of delusions but cannot cut the most subtle, self-grasping mind.

Neither of these extreme views can lead to a true understanding of emptiness. We have to eliminate the inherently existent self entirely while not damaging the existence of the commonly known self. Nagarjuna says:

The nihilistic view only leads to the misery of taking rebirth in the lower realms and eternalism binds us to the suffering of cyclic existence. Therefore only the middle way, which is free from these two extreme views, can lead us to true liberation.

18. Meditation on Emptiness

In the traditional analytical contemplation on emptiness there are three stages:

I   Recognizing the appearance of the inherently existent self.
II Negating the inherently existent self.
III Maintaining the meditation on the emptiness of the inherently existent self.

I. Recognizing the Appearance of the Inherently Existent Self

To be able to identify the appearance of the inherently existent self we must first study and understand intellectually what it means. Then we must go into our experience and observe ourselves to discover how the inherently existent self appears to the self-grasping mind, which is innate, arising habitually from life to life.

The inherently existent self appears as a solid entity, existing from its own side. What we have to understand, however, is that the self is something imputed or labeled by our thought and not something independent of it.

It is difficult to understand that "I" is something that is merely labeled by our thought and it is therefore helpful to have an analogy. Tsonghkapa used the analogy of a snake and rope so that we can understand this easily. Although this analogy is not enough to understand fully how "I" is merely labeled, it is very helpful initially.

When we see a coil of rope in the semi-darkness, we can easily confuse it with a real snake and feel afraid. At that time the rope appears to our mind as if it were a snake but this is only the imputation of our thought. If we go nearer to where the "snake" is, nothing can be found apart from a piece of rope.

Similarly, "I" appears to us on the basis of the aggregates: body, consciousness, sensation, cognition, and compositional factors. It is on the basis of the body that we identify ourselves. When our body is doing something, we naturally project "I" onto it and say "I am walking," "I am eating," "I am hot," and so on.

It is important to observe how "I" appears to the mind. Whenever it appears it does so only on the basis of the aggregates. Therefore the self does not exist in a solid way, from its own side, but is something merely labeled by our self-grasping mind. Due to our not understanding this, however, our mind wrongly views the self as existing from its own side, without depending on being labeled by our mind on the basis of the aggregates. This is what is known as the misconception of self. As soon as our mind views the self as existing from its own side, we start to cling to "me." This gives rise to all other delusions.

When we understand deeply how the self is something that does not exist from its own side but exists in dependence on many other things such as body, consciousness, and so on, this helps us to understand the existence of the commonly known self. We will also realize that the commonly known self can only exist if it does not exist inherently. This makes it easier to see how the commonly known self comes from past lives and goes to the next and how non-virtuous actions from previous lives can affect us now or in the future.

Because we intuitively often feel as if the self is not something separate from this gross body, we find it difficult to accept that the self comes from past lives and does not cease at the time of death but continues. Or sometimes we have the feeling that the self is something completely separate from the body and mind, as if it were a solid entity. This makes it difficult for us to see that the self is something that is merely labeled by our mind.

Once we understand that the self is neither limited to this very material body nor exists separately in a concrete form, but is something merely labeled by our mind on the basis of the aggregates, it is much easier for us to see how it is possible for the self to come from past lives and continuously go on into future lives as the basis of karma and rebirth.

How to Identify the Inherently Existent Self

To be able to identify accurately how the inherently existent self appears to our innate ego-mind, it is not sufficient to have a general understanding of what is meant by inherent self; we need to carefully observe our experience when "I" arises.

According to Tsonghkapa, when we start to observe the "I" we will have many different kinds of experience. Sometimes "I" will appear as if it is sitting inside our body; sometimes it will appear without any shape and color, like empty space; sometimes it will appear in the form of strange shapes and colors; at other times only the aggregates appear, such as form, consciousness, and so on. These are not the genuine appearance of the inherently existent self, so we should not rely on the experience of these appearances.

Then how should we recognize the genuine appearance of what seems to be the inherently existent self? Tsonghkapa suggests we should not simply follow whatever appears to our mind, but should strictly look at how "I" appears on the basis of the aggregates. For example, when we think "I am meditating" or "I am reciting," if we look to see what is happening, we can only find certain activities carried out by our individual aggregates. If we then look further among these aggregates, we can only find separate parts, nothing else. But what happens when these individual aggregates perform an activity is that our mind merely imputes or labels it as "I am doing so and so."

So first the aggregates appear, then the "I" appears. This "I" is not something that exists from its own side but is something that is merely labeled by our mind. If we keep looking further, we will see how the appearance of this imputed "I" intensifies and appears to exist fully from its own side or inherently. When this happens we must be aware of it and simply allow one part of the mind to watch it.

It is very important to recognize the appearance of the inherently existent "I" accurately. If we do not, we will not be able to understand the absence of the "I" as grasped at by our habitual, innate ego-mind when we negate it at a later stage.

When we are watching our habitual, natural thoughts of "I" and "me," we are often tempted to impose our view of what the inherent self might be, rather than simply let it appear to our mind and watch it. This is a mistake we often make. If we impose our idea about "self," then later we will only be able to negate what we imagine to be the inherent self, but we will not be able to negate what our innate ego-mind is actually grasping at. Concerning this point Tsonghkapa said:

> If we do not accurately identify the appearance of the inherent self exactly as it appears to our innate ego-mind, then some kind of inherent self will be left over to be grasped at when we later negate the inherently existent self we have imagined.
>
> Realizing this kind of emptiness cannot help us to cut our innate ego-grasping mind. Therefore what we have to do is first provoke our innate ego-mind within ourself and then simply look at how the "I" appears to it and how it grasps at the self. We should do this with strong mindfulness and deep concentration and not impose any preconceptions about the self. We must carry on this observation of "self" until we clearly and accurately identify the appearance of the inherent self as grasped at by our innate ego-mind.

It is easier for us to see how our innate ego-mind works when we are going through emotional stress or feeling very afraid, for at such times the "I" appears very vividly. So provoke an emotional state of mind by recalling an emotional experience or imagine someone abusing you. Then as soon as anger, fear, or emotional stress arises, we should look into our experience to see how "I" appears.

At that time both the commonly known "I" and the inherently existent "I" will appear to us and we will not be able to distinguish between them. This is because the "I" appears to exist from its own side from every angle that we look at it. We should not worry about this but simply go ahead to discover how the "I" appears to exist inherently. Once we unmistakenly identify the appearance of the inherent self, we then negate it. This will not harm the existence of the commonly known "I."

II. Negating the Inherently Existent Self

After we have clearly recognized the appearance of the inherently existent self through our own experience, the next step is to analyze whether this "I" truly exists and, if it does, how and where it exists.

To do this we use one of many methods of reasoning taught by Lord Buddha and elaborated on by Nagarjuna and his disciples. This particular one is a very effective, clear, and sharp method known as the two-point way of reasoning. In it we negate the inherently existent self by analyzing whether "I" exists among the aggregates or separate from them.

This practice was taught by Buddha in many Mahayana sutras and by Nagarjuna in his main text, *The Treatise on the Middle Way*. Most of Nagarjuna's disciples emphasized this method and Chandrakirti extended it into a seven-point way of reasoning in his *Supplement to Nagarjuna's Treatise on the Middle Way*.

There are three stages in the two-point way of reasoning: (A) reflecting on whether the inherently existent self exists among the aggregates; (B) reflecting on whether the inherently existent self exists separately from them; (C) conclusive reasoning.

First of all we should recall our experience of the way the inherently existent "I" appears and simply observe it. We will see that it appears in many different ways. Sometimes it appears as not being separate from the aggregates, for example, when we think "I am walking." If we look inwardly to see how the "I" appears, it does not appear as something separate from our feet, but when our feet move, it appears that "I" am walking. When we say "I see something" or "I hear something," the "I" does not appear as something separate from our eyes and ears, but when our eyes see or our ears hear, it appears that "I" see or hear. When we say "I know" and "I remember," it appears as not being separate from our mind. On other occasions, when we think "This is my body" or "This is my mind," then the "I" appears to be separate from our body and mind. It appears as if it were a kind of dominator or possessor of the body and mind.

When the "I" appears as the seer, hearer, walker, or thinker, not separate from our aggregates, or when it appears as the possessor of the aggregates, as separate from them, these are all habitual appearances. Our innate ego-mind never analyzes "I" as being the same as the aggregates or separate

from them, but simply takes the appearances for granted and accepts them
without any investigation.

Before we start to investigate, we must be clear that if the "I" does exist
inherently or from its own side, without depending on being imputed by our
thought, in just the way it appears to our innate ego-mind, then it would
exist in the following way: by itself, without depending on anything else.

Bearing this in mind, we then reflect whether the inherently existent self
exists among the aggregates or separately. Here we should look again into
our intuitive feeling to see how the "I" appears to our mind. We will find
that it appears in two different ways: sometimes as not being separate from
the aggregates and sometimes as being separate from them.

A. Reflecting on Whether the Inherently Existent Self
Exists among the Aggregates

If the inherently existent self does exist among the aggregates it must exist
as either one with all of them or as one with body, consciousness, sensation, cognition, or compositional factors (see below).

If it—the inherently existent self—exists as one with all of them simultaneously, then there would be as many separate "I's" as there are aggregates. Checking further, we will see that each of our aggregates has many
parts. Therefore if the "I" exists as one with any of these five individually
defined aggregates, there will be the same problem—multiple selves. For
example, if the "I" exists as one with consciousness, when we break consciousness down into its component parts (see below), again there would
be as many "I's" as there are parts of consciousness.

Let us look at our aggregates more closely to see whether the "I" can be
found among them. Is there anything that can be identified as a solid, separate entity, unchangeable and independent?

To find out whether such an "I" exists in our body, we mentally take it
apart. First we look at the limbs, then all the different parts, breaking them
down into the smallest possible particles. We then take each of these individual parts and check on whether any of them can possibly be identified
as the inherent self. We will see that no matter how far our analysis goes
in this way, nothing can be found that has the same nature as the inherent
"I" would have, if it were to exist.

Everything within our body, from the limbs to the smallest particle, is nothing more than a process of mutual interdependency. Everything exists in dependence on something else. Moreover it does not sound right to think of our limbs as "I." In our everyday life we never think of our head as "I" but as "mine," something that belongs to us.

However, we really feel that this "I" exists somewhere in our body. When we feel afraid, for example, we feel as if it is where our heart is; when we feel sick, as if it exists covering our whole body. At such times we should mentally take our whole body apart to see where this "I" exists and in what form it exists, from the topmost hairs of our head to our toe-nails. We will find nothing but different substances such as blood, hair, bone, and so on. Then looking at each of these elements, we should check if any of them can be identified to be what we think of as "I."

When we analyze whether the "I" is one with the body, we are not just proving that our body is not the "I," our head is not the "I" and so on. We are analyzing whether it is possible for the "I" to exist as it appears to our innate ego-mind, as if existing inherently among the aggregates or separate from them.

Look at how the body exists; examine the whole physical system. From the cells of the skin to those of the marrow, all the cells in our body connect with each other; nothing exists in an independent way. Everything is transient and changes moment by moment. Our body is nothing more than a transient flow due to many causes and conditions. It is impossible for an inherently existent self to exist within the body, for as we see, if such a self existed, it would have to exist without depending on anything else. All of these parts, however, are things that exist due to many causes and conditions.

Now let us move on to check whether this "I" exists in the form of our sensation. First, we must be clear about what sensations are. There is no such thing as a sensation that exists by itself in a specific area, either within our body or our mind. If we look into ourselves to see what sensations look like, they seem to be something rather like an echo that suddenly vibrates due to some stimuli within our consciousness. When we have a headache we may point to some area in our head. However, the sensation of a headache is related to many things within our body and consciousness. Without mind there is no sensation; it occurs in dependence on many other things and relates to our whole system.

Now let us see whether the inherent self exists in the nature of the third aggregate, known as cognition. Like sensation, this aggregate also has no substantial essence. It temporarily occurs in dependence on the position of our organs and the appearance of the external object. Buddha compared the nature of cognition to that of a mirage. When the heat of the sun strikes the desert sands the vision of a mirage occurs. From the distance it looks like something substantial that can be seen, yet in fact there is nothing tangible there.

No inherent "I" can be found in the fourth aggregate, compositional factors. These refer to the mental factors other than sensation and cognition, such as intelligence and desire. This aggregate is related to the other four aggregates in the following way: our consciousness first perceives an object through the form aggregate, for example, eye, nose, tongue, and so on. Then we cognize the object, viewing it as pleasant, unpleasant, or neutral; this mental factor is the aggregate of cognition. From this arises sensation. When we feel a pleasant sensation, desire is generated; when we feel an unpleasant sensation, aversion is generated. Then we take action either to obtain or reject the object. These actions leave karmic imprints on the consciousness and they ripen in future rebirths. So it is through these factors, called the compositional factors, that we engage in actions. In this way this aggregate serves as a link between the other four. Like sensation and cognition, it has no substantial essence; it exists only in dependence on many causes and conditions.

Finally, we may feel that the inherent self exists in the nature of consciousness. If we closely check up on the nature of mind, how it arises and how it changes, we will see that there is no such thing as a mind that exists permanently. What we call mind is merely a collection of events formed by many moments of different thoughts and feelings, each of which arise due to many external and internal causes and conditions.

If we mentally break up our consciousness we are merely left with different types of thought patterns that are constantly changing. Buddha states that the mind or consciousness is like a water-tree. This shows that it has no concrete essence.

When the inherent self appears to our mind, it appears in the form of a concrete, independent, unchangeable entity. It is clear, once we have checked the nature of consciousness, that the inherent self cannot exist in the nature of consciousness.

Therefore, no matter how much further we analyze, no such thing as an inherently existent self can be found among the aggregates. This shows that the self is something imputed from the side of the mind, rather than existing from its own side among the aggregates.

B. Reflecting on Whether the Inherently Existent Self Exists Separately from the Aggregates

If the self exists inherently in exactly the same way as it appears to our innate ego-mind, then it would exist without depending on being imputed by our mind. In this case it would exist by itself without depending on anything else.

So if "I" exists separately from our aggregates, it would exist without depending on any of them or on any other phenomena. It would be a partless, independent, eternal entity. Yet our self is not like that. We experience that what we feel to be "I" or "me" has many parts or aspects. We feel "I am getting old," "I am sick," "I did that," "I am doing this," and so on. Therefore it is obvious that our self is something that has many parts and does various activities, like a very sophisticated machine.

Thus "I" cannot possibly exist as a completely separate and independent entity that is not connected with our aggregates.

In this way we come to realize that the inherent "I" exists neither among the aggregates nor separately from them. We must reflect on these two ways of reasoning again and again with a clear mind and stable concentration. When doing this we must make sure that the inherently existent "I" we are analyzing is not what we intellectualize but what habitually appears to our innate ego-mind. Tsonghkapa says this is very important.

C. Conclusive Reasoning

Conclusive reasoning is the third step, which we take when we realize clearly that the inherently existent "I" exists neither among the aggregates nor separately from them.

Here we must assure ourselves that if the inherent "I" does not exist among the aggregates nor separately from them, it cannot exist at all. No matter how much further we take our analysis there is no third alternative way for the inherent "I" to exist.

We have to reflect alternately on how the inherent "I" cannot exist among the aggregates nor separately from them and yet, if it exists, it must either exist among them or separately from them. There is no other way for it to exist. Therefore it does not exist at all.

We have to investigate whether the inherently existent "I" or "self" exists in every possible way that we suspect it to exist. As we pointed out before, if the inherently existent "I" or "self" does exist, then there are only two possibilities: it must either exist among the aggregates or separately from them. Having checked this thoroughly we come to the point where we cannot find the inherently existent self anywhere at all. At this stage the appearance of the inherently existent self, to which our mind instinctively and intuitively clings, begins to cease and our mind is left with the experience of the emptiness of the inherent self that had previously predominated our mind. Here we stop analyzing and concentrate on the experience for as long as we can. This is called meditation on space-like emptiness. We then repeat the analysis and when, as the result of analysis, we experience the voidness of the inherently existent "I," we should concentrate on it again. We will develop our realization of emptiness through this process of alternating analysis with concentration.

Doubting and Losing the "I"

As we go more deeply into this analysis we will begin to understand through our own experience how an inherently existent "I" cannot exist. Since beginningless time, however, our mind has been habitually grasping at such an "I" and clinging to it. At first, therefore, we will find it very difficult to lose the feeling of this "I" or let go of it.

We will have doubts about the existence of the inherent "I." On the one hand, through sharp reasoning, we clearly see how such an "I" cannot exist. On the other hand, we are afraid that "I" may not exist at all. It is at this stage that we could fall to the extreme view of nihilism if we did not have the guidance of experienced yogis and followed the very skillful ways of reasoning taught by Buddha and Nagarjuna. Many practitioners who meditate on emptiness come out of this stage with an incorrect understanding of it, viewing everything they perceive as being mere illusion.

At an early stage of his life, as if experiencing this kind of emptiness, Tsonghkapa raised the question of whether it was the true emptiness taught by Nagarjuna. He went to one of his main teachers, Lama Umapa, who had had pure visions of Manjushri since his childhood, and requested him to ask Manjushri whether this was the correct understanding of emptiness. Manjushri told Umapa:

> No. The emptiness Tsonghkapa has been experiencing is not the correct understanding of emptiness as taught by Nagarjuna. Tell him not only to negate the inherently existent self, but to give equal priority to maintaining the conventional existence of the self. He should also develop single-pointed devotion to his gurus and see them as being one with his deity. Then he should accumulate merit by offering the mandala and practice purification. He can find the pure understanding of emptiness in the great reliable treatises composed by Nagarjuna and his spiritual sons. By meditating on their methods and following my advice he will soon gain the unmistaken realization of emptiness or the Middle Way.

As Manjushri advised, Tsonghkapa went into solitary retreat to practice and soon gained the pure realization of emptiness. Tsonghkapa himself then had visions of Manjushri and from then on received many teachings from him on sutra and tantra.

In many of his teachings Lama Tsonghkapa stresses:

> Gaining the pure realization of emptiness is not only a matter of being able to negate the inherent existence of the self. It is just as important to maintain the existence of the "I" at the conventional level once the inherently existent "I" has been completely negated through Madhyamika reasoning.
>
> It may happen that the more we negate the inherently existent self, the more we will lose our sense of the existence of the conventional "I." And the more we try to maintain the existence of the conventional "I," the less we will be able to negate the inherently existent self. Thus we fall either to the extreme of nihilism or eternalism and will not be able to attain the realization of the Middle Way.

But if we find that our understanding of the conventional truth [that causes produce their own results and that results depend on their causes] deepens our understanding of the emptiness of inherent existence, and that our understanding of emptiness deepens our acceptance of the conventional truth, then we are approaching the correct understanding of the view of emptiness taught by Buddha and Nagarjuna.

When we feel that our "I" begins to cease we are in danger of falling to the extreme of nihilism, unless we have enough merit, have done enough purification practices, and have the guidance of an experienced teacher.

III. Maintaining the Meditation on the Emptiness of the Inherently Existent Self

Here we shall discuss the practical method of how to meditate on emptiness once we have gained some experience of it.

Some pre–Tsonghkapa yogis say that we should withdraw our mind from all conceptual thought, not analyzing or thinking about anything, and that this is the pure approach to meditation on emptiness.

Others say that we should first have some understanding of emptiness through Madhyamika reasoning and then stop analyzing altogether, completely keeping our mind away from analyzing anything.

But Tsonghkapa points out that in the first approach, although we are meditating in a non-conceptual state, we are not penetrating into the emptiness of inherent existence. In the second approach, although we have some understanding of emptiness, when meditating on it we are no longer penetrating into it. So neither of these is the correct method.

The correct method of meditation on emptiness taught by Tsonghkapa is that first we should gain a correct understanding of emptiness through the analysis of Madhyamika reasoning as presented above. Once we have an experience of emptiness, we should concentrate on it for a while. What is important in this approach is that we should be able to hold the experience of emptiness for as long and strongly as possible.

To enable us to do this, Tsonghkapa recommends two methods: special mindfulness and special vigilance. The mindfulness we develop here is not the same as the one we develop in the practice of single-pointed mind. There it means keeping the picture of the object we have built clearly in our mind.

But keeping the emptiness of inherent existence as the object of our concentration is not sufficient. What is more important is keeping the strength of the experience of emptiness. So we must place more emphasis on keeping and strengthening the experience of emptiness, rather than on merely picturing it. This method is called the practice of special mindfulness.

As soon as the strength of our experience begins to decrease we must be aware of it—this is the special vigilance. What we have to do is concentrate on emptiness for as long as the experience remains strong. When it begins to decrease we must be aware of it and reflect once more on Madhyamika reasoning until we have another experience of emptiness. In this practice, therefore, we alternate between analyzing and concentrating.

When we initially realize the emptiness of inherent existence our mind is still in a conceptual state. Emptiness appears as being separate from our mind. Because of this dualistic appearance our mind is still in a conceptual state. When we experience emptiness, however, we are not merely conceptualizing about it, but are rather penetrating into it. The more we penetrate into emptiness, the more deeply we will experience it. The deeper our experience of emptiness, the more the dualistic appearance between the mind and emptiness will be diminished. Thus analytical meditation on emptiness leads to the direct realization of it, beyond the conceptual state.

Some pre–Tsonghkapa yogis taught a separate technique to help eliminate the dualistic view after emptiness has been realized. Their idea is that if we continually analyze, even after realizing emptiness, this will produce the concept of emptiness, rather than the experience of emptiness itself. This would cause the dualistic view between mind and emptiness to increase. Therefore they say it is important to give up analyzing altogether once we have realized emptiness through reasoning, and remain without having any concept of any kind. This method is called mixing the mind with emptiness.

However Tsonghkapa did not follow this system, he taught a different approach. According to him, even if we have gained realization of emptiness, we need to reflect on the reasonings of emptiness again and again. This will enable us to penetrate more and more deeply, thus increasing our experience of emptiness. We should not stop analyzing altogether, but should alternate between analysis and concentration.

There is a big difference between conceptualization and analytical penetration. When we conceptualize, we merely impose our view, which is based on words and ideas about an object. However, when we analyze and penetrate into the truth of things, we are not imposing an idea, but are trying to expose what reality is to our mind. Therefore through correct analysis we will be able to reach the realization of the truth.

Thus, even after we have reached completely beyond the conceptual state, analytical wisdom will remain. It is analytical wisdom that exposes the truth to our mind. Although at the initial stage it arises from the conceptual state, as it increases it burns away even dualistic appearance and leads our mind completely beyond the conceptual state. In the sutra called *Request by Kasyapa* Buddha explains this as follows:

> O Kasyapa, just as fire arises when two pieces of wood are rubbed against each other, so analytical wisdom arises from the conceptual state. And just as the fire increases and burns away all the wood, analytical wisdom increases and burns away all conceptual states.

Similarly Kamalashila says:

> Through the correct analysis of reasoning, practitioners experience the truth of non-self. As they penetrate more and more into this truth, they eventually reach direct realization of it, totally beyond the conceptual state.

The Actual Meditation Session

The actual meditation on emptiness begins with a visualization of the merit field and purification, as explained below. Having completed this we reflect on the realization of emptiness.

Visualize the merit field in front of you. Think of Buddha Shakyamuni as being one with your guru, sitting on a lotus throne among a great gathering of lineage gurus, deities, bodhisattvas, arhats, dakas, dakinis, and Dharma protectors. The throne is on an enormous fully open lotus at the top of a wish-fulfilling tree, growing from the middle of a large lake full of nectar. The beautiful branches of the tree bear lovely flowers, leaves, and various fruits.

At Buddha Shakyamuni's heart visualize Manjushri, the emanation of all the buddhas' wisdom, sitting on a moon disc and lotus. His right hand is holding a wisdom sword just above the crown of his head. His left hand is in the teaching gesture at his heart and is holding the stem of an utpala flower, which is blooming at his left shoulder. His body is completely golden in color and he is wearing most precious ornaments and very fine clothes. He is smiling.

At Manjushri's heart is a moon disc. Visualize a wisdom sword standing upright in the middle of the moon, with flames rising from the blade. Branching out from the handle are six more swords, pointing horizontally into the six directions with flames moving outward. Inside the handle of the middle sword visualize the syllable *dhi* in golden color, standing upright. Then visualize the six syllables *om ah ra pa tsa na* standing in a clockwise direction on the tip of each horizontal blade. The syllables are radiating brilliant light into the ten directions, purifying all beings, including oneself. Recite the mantra *om ah ra pa tsa na dhi* one hundred times or more.

Reflection on Emptiness

Since beginningless time my mind has been completely dominated by the delusions of the innate ego-grasping mind. It is this inner evil that deceives and fools me; it is not only responsible for all the suffering and unhappiness that I have experienced but it also turns me into a foolish and most cruel being.

Lord Buddha says that the nature of the mind of all beings is pure. This pure nature makes it possible for us to become enlightened. Although it is already within us, we have not yet realized that we have this precious potential.

Under the great temptation of our innate ego-mind we have lost countless opportunities. There is no greater shame for me than to surrender myself carelessly to this merciless inner demon of delusion. If I am truly honest with myself, I must realize that the pure teaching of Lord Buddha is the perfect way. From now on, I shall completely turn away from the temptation of this inner evil and firmly follow the perfect way that the Enlightened One has shown me.

Under the influence of these delusions, my mind is always tempted to cling to the view of self as if it exists inherently, or from its own side. But this is a total deception, imposed on my mind by this clever, cunning demon of delusion. Let me remember how much I have suffered through this temptation.

How glad I am that I can pinpoint the cause of all my suffering through the light of Buddha's teachings. I totally realize that all my suffering is created by this inner evil sitting inside my heart, pretending to be most dear to me.

Because of the kindness of the Enlightened One I now have the wisdom to distinguish the right path from the wrong one; that which is wholesome from that which is evil.

With the wisdom I gain from the perfect teachings of Buddha, I analyze whether the self that appears to me under the influence of my innate ego-mind really exists. Through applying the sharp and profound reasoning of the Middle Way, I come to realize that the view of the inherently existent self cannot be maintained; it is a mere fantasy imposed by my ego-grasping mind.

Since beginningless time my mind has been attached and clinging to my ego, thinking "I" and "me." It is this attachment or self-clinging that brings endless unhappiness to me.

Now I shall thoroughly examine whether my "I" or self does exist inherently, or fully from its own side, as it appears to my innate ego-grasping mind. My "I" has, in fact, no solid nature; it is something that is merely imputed by my own mind on the basis of the aggregates (body, sensation, cognition, compositional factors, and consciousness). However, my "I" always appears to my mind as if it does exist having an inherent nature, or as a concrete entity somewhere within me.

If my "I" were to exist truly, as it appears to my innate ego-grasping mind, as having a concrete entity that is not merely imputed by my mind but exists fully from its own side, then it would exist by itself without depending on anything else. If so, then we should be able to single it out specifically, as soon as we start to analyze to find how and where it exists. There are only two possibilities: it must exist either among the aggregates or separately.

Manjushri

Firstly, let me check up on whether my "I" exists among my aggregates. No matter how far and deeply I analyze, there is no way at all in which this supposed inherently existent "I" can be found among the aggregates. As I closely check, it becomes clear to see how this supposed inherently existent "I" cannot exist within my body aggregate. Nothing within my body can have a concrete nature that exists by itself, without depending on any other component part. Everything within my body—from the tip of my hair to my toes, from my skin to the innermost part of my heart—exists only in dependence on many causes and conditions. The same is true of the other four aggregates.

The sensation aggregate is a series of pleasant, unpleasant, and neutral feelings that arise in dependence on our previous mental states as well as on external objects and internal physical organs. The cognition aggregate, too, is something that arises in dependence on many causes and conditions. It arises from our previous mental state and also from the object of cognition. The aggregate of compositional factors does not exist independently either. The consciousness aggregate is an unceasing flow of moments of consciousness, each moment giving rise to a new one. Each moment of consciousness is dependent on its previous moment of consciousness, hence nothing within these aggregates has a solid entity.

Now I shall check up on whether my "I" exists in a concrete form that can exist either fully from its own side, separately, or in isolation from these aggregates. If my "I" were to exist in such a way, it would be found as having an entirely self-sufficient nature somewhere outside these aggregates and unrelated to them. However, when I put aside these aggregates, no inherently existent "I" can be found anywhere.

As I have thoroughly examined above, my "I" can neither be found to exist as having an inherent nature among my aggregates, nor can it exist separately from them. There is no third possibility.

Hence, my "I" or self is something that is merely imputed by my own mind on the basis of my aggregates and thus is not an inherently existent entity. It is empty of an inherently existent nature, which so vividly and predominantly appears to my innate ego-grasping mind.

O my Guru Manjushri, please bestow your pure wisdom power upon me to be able to achieve the pure realization of emptiness quickly, so that I can benefit all my mother beings and lead them to total liberation from the suffering of cyclic existence.

Having reflected on emptiness, read the following by Lama Tsonghkapa, *The Essence of the Three Principles of Buddha's Teachings*:

I bow down to my kind gurus.

Here I shall explain the essence of all Buddha's teachings: the practice of the great path praised by noble bodhisattvas and the right path for fortunate ones who seek liberation.

You already fortunate ones, who are not tempted by the desire to seek the merely temporary pleasures of samsaric life, but strive to seek a meaningful goal through this precious human rebirth and rely on the right path that pleases Buddha, please listen with a clear mind.

As long as we remain dominated by the desire to seek only samsaric pleasure, unaware of how the whole of samsaric life is in the nature of suffering, we will never achieve the true peace of liberation from the suffering of cyclic existence.

Moreover, it is the insatiable desire for the pleasures of cyclic existence that binds beings to endless suffering.

Therefore, we should first inspire ourselves to transcend cyclic existence.

We have obtained the precious human rebirth this time. How fortunate we are! Yet it is so difficult to find again.

Furthermore, our lifetime is very short—how little time there is for us to achieve a meaningful goal within this lifetime!

If we remind ourselves of this, over and over again, we can turn our mind away from the desire to seek only the pleasures of this very short lifetime, which have little meaning.

The law of cause and effect, which says that virtuous actions bring happiness and non-virtues bring about suffering, is always truthful. Life within cyclic existence is totally subject to endless suffering.

When we deeply realize this, we can then turn our mind away from the desire to seek temporary pleasure anywhere within cyclic existence.

When we experience the enthusiastic aspiration to seek total liberation from cyclic existence, constantly, day and night, with no more desire for the mere pleasures of samsara, we will have generated the true aspiration to transcend cyclic existence.

The aspiration to seek liberation cannot bring forth the perfect bliss of enlightenment if not combined with bodhicitta—the fully compassionate mind, seeing all fellow beings as equal to ourself. Hence, wise ones should inspire themselves to generate bodhicitta, the altruistic mind.

Let us be aware of how all our mother beings helplessly suffer under unbearable conditions: They are swept by the currents of the four mighty rivers of delusion, tightly bound by the chain of the inescapable force of karma, trapped in the iron cage of the misconception of self, engulfed in the total darkness of confusion, powerlessly wandering through the cycle of endless rebirth and death, and unceasingly tormented by the three types of misery. Having realized this, we should generate the aspiration to attain enlightenment for the sake of all our mother beings.

Even though we achieve the true aspiration to seek liberation and have the aspiration to attain enlightenment for the sake of all our fellow beings, without realizing the ultimate truth we cannot cut the root of the suffering of cyclic existence. Therefore we should strive to understand the truth of interdependent arising.

Those who see the truth of the law of cause and effect within all phenomena, in cyclic existence as well as beyond it, and annihilate the false view of self, held by misconception, have entered the right path that pleases Buddha.

As long as we find that emptiness and the law of cause and effect are unrelated in such a way that, in appearance, things arise from causes and conditions, however, in our understanding of emptiness we cannot assert anything, we have not yet realized the true understanding of emptiness taught by Buddha.

When we are able to eliminate the misconception of self completely, at the same time as we see the truth of the law of cause and effect, then our understanding of emptiness is complete.

Understanding the law of cause and effect helps us to eliminate the extreme view of inherent existence, and understanding the emptiness of inherent existence helps us to eliminate the extreme view of nihilism. If we realize emptiness in such a way that things are empty of inherent existence because they are dependent on their causes and conditions, and that things do exist conventionally because they lack an inherently existent nature, only then will we not be deprived of our true understanding of emptiness by either of the two extreme views—nihilism and eternalism.

O my spiritual son or daughter, when you understand the essence of these three principles of Buddha's teachings thoroughly, please devote your life to practicing them in solitude and with unceasing effort to achieve the most meaningful goal.

19. Meditations on the Three Deities

Meditation on Avalokiteshvara

The three deities are the embodiment of Buddha's compassion, wisdom, and spiritual power. Avalokiteshvara is the embodiment of Buddha's compassion. Here we present a meditation on Avalokiteshvara:

To begin, think that all sentient beings gathered around us have tremendous faith in Avalokiteshvara, the deity of compassion. Visualize in the space above our head and facing in the same direction as we do, Avalokiteshvara, sitting in the lotus position, with one face and four arms, radiating white light, full of compassion for all sentient beings. He wears a jeweled crown and other ornaments such as necklace, shining silk clothes, and holds a wish-fulfilling jewel in his joined hands at his heart level, representing his body, mind, speech, and power to fulfill all the needs of sentient beings.

In his second right hand he holds a pure lotus representing his compassion; in his second left hand a crystal rosary which represents crystal-clear wisdom. At his heart is a clear moon-disc and in the middle of it is the letter *hri* which represents the seed syllable from which the deity Avalokiteshvara arises to benefit us all; around it surrounds the mantra *om ma ni pe me hum*, in white color.

This mantra has six letters, the first one is *om* indicating the purity of Buddha's speech, mind, and body. The second and third letters *ma* and *ni* together mean fulfilling joy. The fourth and fifth letters *pe* and *me* together indicate the lotus. The sixth letter *hum* shows the omniscient mind.

After visualizing Avalokiteshvara in this manner, reflect on the boundless qualities of Avalokiteshvara's compassion and wisdom. Through this reflection, when strong faith in him arises in the mind, start the recitation of the mantra: *om ma ni pe me hum* (following the visualization). Simultaneously, think that a pure nectar comes from the seed syllable *hri* and from the mantra garland around it; this enters the body through the crown, purifying all delusions and negativities of body, mind, and speech. These negativities are in the form of black ink which seeps from the pores throughout your body. At the same time, nectars enter into the bodies of all sentient beings around us, purifying their delusions and negativities in the same way.

Lastly, our own and all sentient beings' bodies become as clean as stainless crystal and gain the same qualities as Avalokiteshvara. We can recite the mantra as many times as we wish, at our leisure. At the end, say the following prayer:

With this virtue may I achieve the state of Avalokiteshvara; may I be able to lead all sentient beings to attain that state.

Meditation on Manjushri

Buddha's omniscient wisdom emanates in the form of the diety known as Manjushri; he has the special power to bestow blessings for gaining wisdom within our minds.

In this meditation, we visualize Manjushri in the space above our head, facing the same direction as we face. He is in a shining golden color, radiating rays of light in the ten directions. Seated in the lotus position, he wears a jeweled crown; his hair in blue-black color is worn in a top-knot. He has all jeweled necklaces and ornaments and is wearing shining silk clothes. Full of wisdom, he holds a wisdom-sword in his right hand with his arm raised above his head and has a book of the Perfection Sutra in his left hand held at his heart level.

This visualization is followed by recitation of the mantra: *om ah ra pa tsa na dhi,* meaning: To pay respect to you who brings wisdom maturity to the minds of all sentient beings. While reciting this, think that pure nectar comes from the mantra on the moon-disc at the heart of Manjushri and enters into the body through the crown. This nectar purifies our ignorance in the form of black ink, coming out through all the pores of our skin, and our body becomes a fully purified light form. The mind shines in boundless wisdom light-rays. These light-rays spread throughout the entire world, purifying the minds of all sentient beings.

At the end of the recitation, say the following prayer:

You, compassionate Manjushri, please purify our ignorance with your boundless shining wisdom and bestow upon us the wisdom fully understanding the meaning of all Buddha's teachings.

Meditation on Vajrapani

Vajrapani represents the wrathful deity aspect—the embodiment of all Buddha's spiritual power. He has endless power to free us from obstacles caused by internal, external, and secret maras—negative powers. The "internal mara" is our delusion; "secret mara" is an imbalance of wind energy within the body; and "external mara" is negative influence coming externally to hinder us from improving our spiritual practice.

Visualize Vajrapani in the space about our head, facing in the same direction as we do. He stands upon a sun-disc on a lotus; his body in blackish-blue shining color, showing a wrathful form out of full compassion. He holds a vajra in his right hand raised to the sky. His left hand is in the warning position at his heart level. Wearing a jeweled crown and all other ornaments, with strings of jewels and a tiger-skin at his waist hanging to his feet.

Visualize the letter *hum* surrounded by the mantra *om vajra pani hum* on a sun-disc at his heart. Imagine pure nectar coming from the mantra: it fills all the body, purifying all negative karma—illness, whatever we might have, evil influences—in the form of black ink, impure blood and pus and various kinds of insect forms coming out of all the pores of the skin. Our body becomes pure with the protection of vajra-skin: skin built with vajras.

Conclude the meditation with the formal prayers:

Please free us from all negative powers and evil influences and clear all obstacles that we may be able to complete our practice; and please provide us with all the internal and external conducive facilities to practice the Buddha's path, and bestow upon us complete fortune to achieve enlightenment.

Appendix:
Prayers in Tibetan Phonetics and English

Taking Refuge and Generating Bodhicitta

Sang gyä chö dang tsog kyi chog nam la
jang chub bar du dag ni kyab su chi
dag gi jin sog gyi pai sö nam kyi
dro la pän chir sang gyä drub bar shog

I go for refuge until I am enlightened
To the buddhas, the Dharma, and the Highest Assembly.
From the virtuous merit that I collect
By practicing giving and other perfections,
May I attain the state of a buddha
To be able to benefit all sentient beings.

Purifying the Place

Tam chä du ni sa zhi dag
seg ma la sog me pa dang
lag til tar nyam be dur yäi
rang zhin jam por nä gyur chig

May all lands completely become
As smooth as the surface of lapis lazuli
And as even as the palm of my hand
Without any defects such as thorns and rubble.

Blessing the Offerings

Hla dang mi yï chö pä dzä
ngö su sham dang yi kyi trül
kün zang chö trin la na mä
nam khä kham kün khyab gyur chig

May the entire realm of space be filled
With the supreme clouds of Samantabhadra's offerings
And with the offerings of gods and humans,
Both those that are physically offered
And those visualized.

Mantra for Blessing the Offerings

om namo bhagawate, bändze sara parma da na, tathagataya, arhate
samyak sambuddhaya, tayata, om bändze bändze, maha bändze, maha
tedza bändze, maha biya bändze, maha bodhicitta bändze, maha
bodhi mando pa sam da ma na bändze, sarwa karma ah wa ra na bi
sho da na bändze soha

The Seven Limb Prayer

Ji nye su dag chog chü jig ten na
du sum sheg pa mi yi seng ge kün
dag gyi ma lü de dag tam che la
lü dang ngag yi dang wä chag gyo

I bow down respectfully with my body, speech, and faithful mind,
To all Tathagatas in the ten directions,
Those who have already reached the Tathagata state,
Those who are reaching it at present
And those Tathagatas still to come.

Zang po chöd päi mün lam tob dag gi
gyal wa tam che yi kyi ngön sum du

zhing gi dül nye lü rab tü pa yi
gyal wa kün la rab tu chag tsel lo

Through the power of Samantabhadra's prayers,
May all buddhas manifest vividly in my mind.
I prostrate to them, multiplying my body
As many times as there are atoms of the earth.

Dül chig teng na dül nye sang gyä nam
sang gyä sä kyi ü na zhug pa dag
de tar chö kyi ying nam ma lü pa
tam che gyal wa dag gi gang war mö

In each atom I visualize as many buddhas as there are atoms,
Surrounded by countless bodhisattvas.
Thus, all space is filled with buddhas and bodhisattvas.

De dag ngag pa mi ze gya tso nam
yang yi yen lag gya tsöi dra kün gyi
gyal wa kün gyi yön ten rab jö ching
de war sheg pa tam che dag gi tö

I praise all buddhas through magnificent chanting
Expressing the great ocean of their excellent qualities.

Me tog dam pa treng wa dam pa dang
sil nyän nam dang jug pa dug chog dang
mar me chog dang dug pö dam pa yi
gyäl wa de dag la ni chöd par gyi

To all buddhas I make offerings of various pure flowers, flower
    garlands,
Of music, anointing oils, magnificent light, and fragrant incense.

Na za dam pa nam dang dri chog dang
che ma fur ma ri rab nyam pa dang

köd pa kyä par fag pei chog kün gye
gyal wa de dag la ni chöd par gyi

I make offerings to them of fine garments, perfume, and potpourri,
Piled high as Mount Meru and arranged in the most beautiful way.

Chöd pa gang nam la me gya che wa
de dag gyal wa tam che la yang mö
zang po chöd la de pä tob dag gyi
gyal wa kün la chag tsel chöd par gyi

I visualize the highest and most extensive offerings
And offer them with great faith to all buddhas.
I prostrate to the buddhas and make offerings to them,
Following the deeds of the great bodhisattva, Samantabhadra.

Död chag zhe dang ti mug wang gi ni
lü dang ngag dang de zhin yi kyi kyang
dig pa dag gi gyi pa ji chi pa
de dag tam che dag gi so sor shag

I confess to you, buddhas,
Whatever negative actions I have done
Due to the power of anger, desire, and ignorance.

Chog chui gyal wa kün dang sang gyä sä
rang gyäl nam dang lob dang mi lob dang
dro wa kün gyi sö nam gang la yang
de dag kün gyi je su dag yi rang

I rejoice in the merit of all the buddhas in the ten directions,
Of the great bodhisattvas and Pratyeka buddhas,
Those who have attained arhathood,
Those who have entered the path to arhathood,
And all other beings.

Gang nam chog chüi jig ten drön ma dag
jang chub rim par sang gyä ma chag nye
gön po de dag dag gi tam che la
kor lo la na med pa kor war kül

I make requests to all Great Protectors or buddhas
To turn the highest wheel of Dharma,
As the light dispelling the darkness of the beings in the ten directions
To lead them gradually to the enlightened state.

Nya ngyän da tön gang zhe de dag la
dro wa kün la fen zhing de wä chir
kel pa zhing gi dül nye zhug par yang
dag gi tel mo rab jar söl war gyi

I make requests to those buddhas
Intending to pass into parinirvana,
To live long, for as many eons as there are atoms of the earth,
In order to benefit all beings.

Chag tsel wa dang chöd ching shag pa dang
je su yi rang kül zhing söl wa yi
ge wa chung zä dag gi ji sag pa
tam che dag gi jang chub chir ngo wo

I dedicate whatever merit I have gained
From prostrating, making offerings,
Confessing my negativities,
Rejoicing in the virtue of others,
Requesting the buddhas to turn the wheel of Dharma,
Requesting them to live long,
So that I may attain enlightenment
For the sake of all beings.

The Mandala Offering Prayer

Om vajra bhumi ah hung   wang chen ser gyi sa zhi
Om vajra rekhe ah hung   chi chag ri kor yug gyi kor wä ü su
ri gyal po ri rab (1)
shar lü pag po (2)   lho dzam bu ling (3)
nub ba lang chö (4)   jang dra mi nyän (5)
lü (6) dang lü pag (7)   nga yab (8) dang nga yab zhän (9)
yo dän (10) dang lam chog dro (11)
dra mi nyän (12) dang dra mi nyän gyi da (13)
*rinpoche ri wo (14)   pag sam gyi shing (15)   do jö ba (16)   ma mö
    pa yi lo tog (17)*

Om vajra bhumi ah hung, greatly powerful golden ground.
Om vajra rekhe ah hung, at the outermost limit a circular iron
    mountain chain surrounds Mount Meru, king of mountains (1).
In the east is the continent Lüpagpo (2)
In the south the continent Dzambuling (3)
In the west the continent Balangchö (4)
In the north the continent Draminyän (5)
At the two sides of the eastern continent are two subcontinents Lü
    (6) and Lüpag (7)
At the two sides of the southern continent are two subcontinents
    Ngayab (8) and Ngayabzhän (9)
At the two sides of the western continent are two subcontinents
    Yoden (10) and Lamchogdro (11)
At the two sides of the northern continent are two subcontinents
    Draminyän (12) and Draminyängyida (13).
Precious mountain (4), wish-granting tree (15), wish-fulfilling cow
    (16), and uncultivated crops (17).

*Kor lo rin po che (18)   norbu rin po che (19)   tzün mo rin po che
    (20)   lon po rin po che (21)   lang po rin po che (22)   ta chog rin
    po che (23)   mag po rin po che (24)   ter chen pö yi bum pa (25)*

Precious wheel (18), precious jewel (19), precious queen (20), precious minister (21), precious elephant (22), precious horse (23), precious general (24), and great treasure vase (25).

Geg ma (26)   treng wa ma (27)   lu ma (28)   gar ma (29)   me tog ma (30)   dug pö ma (31)   nang säl ma (32)   dri chab ma (33)

Goddess of grace (26), goddess of garlands (27), goddess of song (28), goddess of dance (29), goddess of flowers (30), goddess of incense (31), goddess of light (32), and goddess of perfume (33).

Nyi ma (34)   da wa (35)   rin po che dug (36)   chog la nam par gyä wä gyäl tsän (37)   ü su lha dang mi päl jor pün sum tsog pa (38)

Sun (34), moon (35), precious umbrella (36), and banner of victory in every direction (37),
And in the center, all the prosperity and possessions of gods and humans (38).

Ma tsang wa me pa tzang zhing yid du wong wa di dag drin chen tza wa dang gyü par chä pä päl dän lama dam pa nam dang kye per du yang lama sha kya thub pa lha tsog kor dang chä pä nam la zhing gam ül war gyio

This magnificent and glorious collection, encompassing all prosperity and goodness,
I offer to you, my most kind root Guru,
To all other holy lineage gurus,
In particular to you, Buddha Shakyamuni,
Together with the entire assembly of the merit field.

Tug je dro way dön du zhe su söl zhe nay dag sog dro wa mar gyur nam kay ta dang nyam pay sem chen tam chay la tug tsay wa chen pö go nay jin gyi lab tu söl.

Please accept this offering for the welfare of all sentient beings,
And, having accepted it, with your great kindness,
Please bestow your blessings and inspiration on me
And all mother beings throughout space.

Short Mandala Offering

Sa zhi pö kyi jug shing me tog tram
ri rab ling shi nyi dä gyän pa di
sang gyä shing du mig te ül war gyi
dro kün nam dag zhing la chö par shog

By virtue of offering to you, assembly of buddhas
Visualized before me, this mandala built on a base,
Resplendent with flowers, sprinkled with perfumed water,
Adorned with Mount Meru and the four continents,
As well as the sun and moon.
May all sentient beings share in its good effects.

Om idam guru ratna mandalakam niryatayami

I send forth this jeweled mandala to you, precious Gurus.

Glossary

ABHIDARMA. (Skt) Buddha's teachings in which the wisdom realizing the characteristics of phenomena is extensively described.

ARHAT. (Skt) One who has reached beyond rebirth in cyclic existence.

ARYA BEING. One who has gained direct realization of emptiness.

ARYADEVA. A chief disciple of Nagarjuna, fourth century CE.

ASANGA. Founder of the Chittamatra, or Mind-Only School, fifth century CE.

BINDHU. (Skt) Energy drop, which is composed of the essence of white energy from the father and red energy from the mother.

BODHICITTA. (Skt) Altruistic mind.

BODHISATTVA. (Skt) One who truly generates bodhicitta.

BRAHMA. (Skt) King of the form realm.

BUDDHA. (Skt) An enlightened being; Tathagata; one of the Three Jewels.

BUDDHA SHAKYAMUNI. The historical Buddha who lived about two and a half thousand years ago.

BUDDHA NATURE. The potential for achieving enlightenment; tathagata essence.

CHAKRA (Skt). Literally means circle and refers to particular psychic nerve centers, which have the shape of a wheel. It is a very important object of meditation in tantric practice.

CYCLIC EXISTENCE. The cycle of death and rebirth under the power of delusion and karma; samsara (Skt). See the three realms.

DAKA/DAKINI. (Skt) Male/female Buddhist yogi who has achieved high realizations on the tantric path.

DEITY. Refers to the symbolic form of a pure being manifested from Buddha's wisdom; yidam (Tib), meaning the object of our devotion.

DELUSION. Misconception and its resultant afflicted states of mind, for example, anger, jealousy, attachment, and so on.

DESIRE REALM. One of the three realms of cyclic existence mentioned in Buddhist scriptures. It is the realm where beings enjoy five external sense objects: form, sound, smell, touch, and taste. There are six realms within this realm: god, demigod, and human—the happy or higher realms; animal, hungry ghost, and hell realms—the unhappy or lower realms.

DHARMA. (Skt) This has many meanings. Here it is the positive means whereby we protect ourselves from suffering; the pure path taught by Buddha; one of the Three Jewels.

DHARMAKAYA. (Skt) The pure inner state of enlightened beings, which has two aspects: pure wisdom and the pure ultimate nature of Buddha's mind.

DHARMA PROTECTOR. One who has achieved higher powers through practice of the path and dedicates him or herself to protect those who follow the right path.

DIGNAGA. An Indian Buddhist logician who lived in the fifth century CE. He is considered to be the father of Buddhist logic.

DROMTÖN RINPOCHE. The chief disciple of Atisha in Tibet.

EON. Period consisting of many millions of years.

FIVE AGGREGATES. The parts of which we are composed, which serve as the basis for the identification of the self or "I." They are: form, sensation, cognition, compositional factors, and consciousness.

FIVE HEINOUS CRIMES. Killing one's father, mother, or an arhat; attempting to wound a Tathagata; causing division among the Sangha.

FORMLESS REALM. This is even further beyond the desire realm than the form realm. Here beings have renounced even form and exist only within the stream of consciousness. Although they have temporarily abandoned attachment to form pleasures, the mind is still bound by subtle desire and attachment to mental states and ego, therefore they are within samsara.

FORM REALM. One of the three realms of cyclic existence, beyond the desire realm. Here beings have renounced the enjoyment of external sense objects yet still have attachment to internal form, that is, their own body and mind.

GELUG TRADITION. The system of the whole of Buddha's teachings, both sutra and tantra, established by Lama Tsonghkapa in the fourteenth century. Gelug means stainless and complete system of practice.

GESHE. (Tib) Originally one who is qualified as a spiritual friend. In the Gelug tradition it is now used as a title for one who has mastered Buddhist philosophy and meditational techniques.

GOD REALM. There are three kinds of god realm: one is in the desire realm, the others are in the form and formless realms.

GURU. (Skt) Spiritual master; lama (Tib).

GUHYASAMAJA. (Skt) The essential tantric practice at the highest level of tantra. It is based on meditation on a specific tantric deity named Guhyasamaja, meaning collection or containing the whole essence of highest tantric practice.

HELL REALMS. The lowest of the realms in the desire realm.

HERUKA TANTRA. (Skt) One of the essential practices of highest tantra based on meditation on a particular deity called Heruka, meaning inseparability of ultimate reality and the most subtle clear wisdom.

HIGHER REALMS. The god, demigod, and human realms.

HUNGRY GHOST REALM. Beings born here suffer from the lack of food, drink, and shelter.

ILLUSORY BODY. A high state of pure subtle body achieved through tantric practice.

KADAM. (Tib) The pure method of taking all Buddha's teachings strictly as personal instructions in order to train the mind.

KADAMPA LAMA. (Tib) A lama who follows the Kadam tradition, established by Atisha in the eleventh century.

KARMA. (Skt) Action of body, speech, and mind. This serves as the seed of future experience by planting potentials on our stream of consciousness for future results.

KAGYU TRADITION. A tradition of practicing both Buddha's sutra and tantra teachings, based on an unbroken or pure transmission from Buddha. This tradition was established by the great Tibetan yogi, Marpa the Translator, who lived in the eleventh century.

LAMA (Tib). This is used as a title for one's own spiritual teacher; guru (Skt).

LINEAGE HOLDER. One who has received the transmission of important teachings from Buddha, has followed and practiced them, and transmits them to others.

LOWER REALMS. The animal, hungry ghost, and hell realms.

MERIT. Positive energy.

MERIT FIELD. Manifestation of buddhas, bodhisattvas, and our own spiritual teacher as the objects of our devotion.

MILAREPA. Tibetan yogi who lived 1040–1123. He was the chief disciple of Marpa and famous for his songs.

NAGARJUNA. Born in the first century BCE and lived for six hundred years. He was the founder of the Madhyamika or Middle Way School.

NIRVANA. (Skt) Liberation from cyclic existence.

PRANA. (Skt) Psychic wind energy, which flows through our psychic nerves.

PRATYEKA BUDDHA. (Skt) A Hinayana arhat who has achieved liberation from cyclic existence mainly through practice in solitude.

PRETA REALM. (Skt) Hungry ghost realm.

PURE LANDS. Realms beyond samsara.

RINPOCHE. (Tib) Literally precious one. In the Tibetan tradition it is generally used for one who is a recognized reincarnate lama; a respectful title used for one's own spiritual master.

ROOT GURU. In the context of the gradual path, our root guru is the one from whom we mainly receive teachings on this practice. Therefore, if we receive many different teachings from different teachers, we have many root gurus.

RUPAKAYA. (Skt) The physical manifestation of an enlightened being.

SAKRAVARTEN KING. (Skt) Literally, Sakravarten means those who rule by the power of the wheel. These were powerful historical kings who lived before the time of Buddha Shakyamuni.

SAMANTABHADRA. (Skt) A great bodhisattva who benefited countless beings by making numberless, priceless offerings to buddhas and bodhisattvas over many eons.

SAMATHA. (Skt) The fully trained state of the meditative mind, calm, clear, stable, and flexible.

SANGHA. (Skt) Those who are purely devoted to the virtuous path taught by Buddha. These are our best spiritual friends; one of the Three Jewels.

SAMSARA. (Skt) See cyclic existence.

SIX REALMS. See desire realm.

SRAVAKA ARHAT. (Skt) One who has achieved liberation from cyclic existence on the Hinayana Path mainly with the help of a spiritual guide.

STUPA. (Skt) A monument symbolizing Buddha's inner qualities.

SUTRA. (Skt) Teachings of Buddha, which are based on the three trainings of morality, concentration, and wisdom, and the six perfections.

TANTRA. (Skt) Literally means continuity or the process of transforming our impure state of body, speech, and mind into a pure state. A great many fine skills of transformation are taught using the practice of deity yoga and meditation on the inner chakras, channels, wind energy, energy drops, and so on.

TATHAGATA. (Skt) One who reaches the highest realization of ultimate truth or emptiness; Buddha.

TATHAGATA ESSENCE. The ultimate nature of beings, which serves as the foundation for achieving the state of a Tathagata; buddha nature.

TATHAGATA REALM. Refers to an inner realm or state, meaning the highest realization that an enlightened being has entered into.

THREE CIRCLES. Here they refer to an action, the object of an action, and the doer of an action.

THREE JEWELS. These refer to Buddha, the Enlightened One; the Dharma, the pure path shown by Buddha; the Sangha, those who are purely devoted to following this path.

THREE REALMS. The desire realm, the form realm, and the formless realm, all within cyclic existence.

THREE TRAININGS. Training in morality, concentration, and wisdom.

TSONGHKAPA. A great Tibetan yogi, 1357–1419, widely considered to be an emanation of Manjushri. He received all the pure transmissions of both sutra and tantra from most famous contemporary scholars and yogis in Tibet, and established a complete and pure tradition of practicing tantras and sutras within one path, stage by stage. This system is known as the Gelug tradition.

VAJRADHARA. (Skt) Fundamental tantric deity who represents the highest attainment of tantric practice.

VINAYA. (Skt) Buddha's teachings on discipline.

VIRTUE. Positive states of mind. For the five different types of virtue see pages 15–16.

YAMANTAKA. (Skt) Destroyer of inner evil.

About the Author

Geshe Namgyal Wangchen was born in Tibet in 1934 and educated at Drepung Monastary (the largest monastic educational institution in the world). In 1959, along with His Holiness the Dalia Lama and 100,000 other Tibetans, he fled the Chinese occupation of his homeland. During the 1980's he began teaching western students in London, England. He now lives and teaches in the re-established Drepung Monastery in India.

About Wisdom Publications

Wisdom Publications, a nonprofit publisher, is dedicated to making available authentic works relating to Buddhism for the benefit of all. We publish books by ancient and modern masters in all traditions of Buddhism, translations of important texts, and original scholarship. Additionally, we offer books that explore East-West themes unfolding as traditional Buddhism encounters our modern culture in all its aspects. Our titles are published with the appreciation of Buddhism as a living philosophy, and with the special commitment to preserve and transmit important works from Buddhism's many traditions.

To learn more about Wisdom, or to browse books online, visit our website at www.wisdompubs.org.

You may request a copy of our catalog online or by writing to this address:

Wisdom Publications
199 Elm Street
Somerville, Massachusetts 02144 USA
Telephone: 617-776-7416
Fax: 617-776-7841
Email: info@wisdompubs.org
www.wisdompubs.org

The Wisdom Trust

As a nonprofit publisher, Wisdom is dedicated to the publication of Dharma books for the benefit of all sentient beings and dependent upon the kindness and generosity of sponsors in order to do so. If you would like to make a donation to Wisdom, you may do so through our website or our Somerville office. If you would like to help sponsor the publication of a book, please write or email us at the address above.

Thank you.

Wisdom is a nonprofit, charitable 501(c)(3) organization affiliated with the Foundation for the Preservation of the Mahayana Tradition (FPMT).